# EVERLASTING
# GOSPEL
## EVER-CHANGING
# WORLD

# EVERLASTING GOSPEL
## EVER-CHANGING WORLD

INTRODUCING
JESUS
TO A
SKEPTICAL
GENERATION

## Jon Paulien

**Pacific Press® Publishing Association**
Nampa, Idaho
Oshawa, Ontario, Canada
www.pacificpress.com

Cover design by Lars Justinen
Illustration work by Lars Justinen
Inside design by Steve Lanto

Additional copies of this book are available by calling toll-free
1-800-765-6955 or online at http://www.adventistbookcenter.com.

Library of Congress Cataloging-in-Publication Data

Paulien, Jon, 1949-
Everlasting gospel, ever-changing world / Jon Paulien.
    p. cm.
ISBN 13: 978-0-8163-2262-6 (paperback)
ISBN 10: 0-8163-2262-7
1. Seventh-day Adventists—Membership. 2. Evangelistic work.
3. Secularism.  I. Title.

BX6154.P325 2008
286.7'32—dc22

2007047380

08 09 10 11 12 • 5 4 3 2 1

# Contents

# Introduction

By the 1980 General Conference Session in Dallas, it had become clear to church leaders that momentous changes were occurring in Western society. Fewer and fewer people were going to church or were even interested in spiritual things. Evangelistic strategies that had once drawn hundreds and baptized dozens were now falling flat. Throughout the '70s repeated attempts to energize church pastors and members with slogans and global campaigns had worked primarily in places where things were already going well. As the decade drew to a close, it seemed clear that something big and threatening was happening in the Western world and that church leaders needed to understand what was going on.

Actually, religious practices had been in decline throughout the Western world (Europe, North America, Australia, and New Zealand) for the past one hundred years. Sociologists identified this decline as a process of secularization. People were living their lives with less and less reference to God. Fewer and fewer were finding church attendance to be a meaningful use of time. Westerners were not becoming atheists as such; they simply no longer considered God to be an active and meaningful part of their everyday lives.

The 1980 General Conference Session, therefore, established a Committee on Secularism, under the leadership of Humberto Rasi. The committee was to study the changes that were taking place and recommend strategies to reach secular people with the Adventist message. Committee members saw the need to explore the literature on secularization and the strategies that various churches, both inside and outside the Seventh-day Adventist Church, had attempted in order to reach out to secular people. But since church leaders are busy people, the committee decided around 1982 to hire me to do some of the research for them, which expanded my interest in the topic. The major product of the committee's work was a book, *Meeting the Secular Mind,* which had some impact on the church but was, perhaps, a bit too technical for most people.* So, the average Adventist remained fairly unaware of the changes taking place in society and the church's response to them.

In 1986 I was invited by Elder Don Schneider, then president of the Rocky Mountain Conference (Colorado and Wyoming), to replace a camp-meeting speaker who couldn't come at the last minute. On the phone, we settled the main speaking slots that I would fill. Then Elder Schneider asked, "Would you be willing to take a seminar in the afternoons? We have an hour-and-a-half slot each afternoon when people have a choice of several topics to attend. I'd appreciate it if you could take one of those seminars and enhance the variety of offerings we can present."

"Sure, I'd be happy to," I replied.

"Great," he said. "Do you have a topic you think the people would be interested in? How about something on the book of Revelation?" (Everybody seems to want me to talk about the book of Revelation!)

I thought for a moment. "Well, there *is* something I have been spending a lot of time with lately, and I'd like to try it out on a live audience. It is the issue of secularism and how that is affecting our churches and their attempts to reach out to their communities. I could talk about what is going on in the outside world and what we can do about it."

Elder Schneider seemed rather skeptical. "I don't know. That sounds like something our young people would be interested in. But camp meeting, at least during the week, attracts mostly retirees, and I'm not sure you'd get more than eight or nine people to attend a seminar on secularism."

"Well, I'd like to try it and see how it goes."

"Suit yourself," he replied, with the usual twinkle in his voice. "If worst comes to worst, we will both know a topic we won't want to do next time!"

To Elder Schneider's shock, some fifty people attended the seminar on the first afternoon—five times as many as he expected. The next afternoon

---

* Humberto Rasi and Fritz Guy, eds., *Meeting the Secular Mind: Some Adventist Perspectives,* Selected Working Papers of the Committee on Secularism of the General Conference of Seventh-day Adventists (Berrien Springs, Mich.: Andrews University Press, 1985).

about a hundred people came. The third day we moved to a larger room, and a hundred and fifty people showed up. Elder Schneider and I realized that the topic was striking a nerve, even in the older generation, whose children and grandchildren were becoming secular. But as word of the seminar got around, young adults and middle-aged Adventists who lived in the area took time off from work and drove to the campground to get in on the seminar. The emotion I sensed most from those attending the seminar was hope— hope that the church was beginning to grapple with issues that they knew were real even though they didn't fully understand what was going on.

I took courage from that camp meeting and began to make the study of secularism and its impact on Adventist faith and practice a major focus of my ministry. In camp meeting after camp meeting, and in many pastors' conferences, the same kind of excitement prevailed. Better yet, each speaking appointment provided me with real-life illustrations of various concepts. Critiques of my presentations also identified weak spots and helped me make changes. The resulting material was published as *Present Truth in the Real World*, in 1993.

I wrote that book specifically with the North American situation in mind, the one that I knew best. But as the book circulated around the world, it seemed to resonate just as much in Western Europe as in North America, just as much in Eastern Europe as in Western Europe. Even more surprising, the book resonated in places like Africa, India, Korea, and the islands of the Pacific. This indicated two things:

1. Secularization is far more widespread than most of us thought. Through television, movies, music, and the Internet, Western ideas and practices are rapidly becoming the "norm" nearly everywhere.
2. The basic principles of outreach shared in *Present Truth in the Real World* were reasonably universal and could be applied to new situations as they arose.

In the sense that it deals with the same issues, *Everlasting Gospel, Everchanging World* is a revised edition of my earlier book. But in another sense, it is a completely fresh reworking of the subject in light of the rise and increasing dominance of what I call "postmodern" secularism. To all those who love people and long to reach them with the gospel no matter what effort or cost must be expended, this book is dedicated to you.

# CHAPTER ONE

# God Meets People Where They Are

When we think of "mission," we usually think of people in faraway places whose language and culture are radically different from our own. We don't think of our neighbors who speak our language and live in circumstances similar to our own. But the average Western Christian would find it easier to share his or her faith in Fiji, Indonesia, or Zimbabwe than in New York, Sydney, or London. So, it is time we think seriously about mission to the mainstream West.

Adventists today are as committed to public evangelism as they have ever been. Satellite evangelism, prophecy seminars, and/or a variety of bridge programs (stop-smoking plans, weight-control programs, family finance seminars) occur annually in most Adventist churches. And we continue to reach people with the gospel message. There are even a few major success stories. But we need to be honest with ourselves. The typical Adventist church is not changing its local community, much less the world, through its activities. We aren't significantly affecting the heart of Western culture. Is this lack of impact our problem or the problem of the culture? Is mainstream Western culture just naturally impervious to the gospel? Or are we missing something?

## The gospel comes in context

Many people would prefer leaving the audience out of consideration in outreach. They feel that we shouldn't have to meet secular people on their own terms. They would agree with sentiments like these: "Truth is truth, and it shouldn't be watered down to please those who aren't following God. Our job is to present the message as we know and appreciate it, and if they don't like it, that's their problem. Isn't it the Holy Spirit's role to bridge the gap between people?" Evangelism is " 'Not by might nor by power, but by My Spirit,' / Says the LORD of hosts" (Zechariah 4:6, NKJV).

Of course, the Holy Spirit is essential to all effective outreach. To attempt to carry out any of the suggestions in this book without the guidance and support of the Spirit would be absolute foolishness. The Holy Spirit can certainly communicate directly to any human being regardless of his background! But Romans 1:18–20 indicates that the Spirit's work is generally quite limited in content. The Spirit does not normally function as a substitute for human effort (see Romans 10:14).

The biblical evidence underlines the importance of careful attention to the cultural horizons of the audience. And Ellen White counsels, "Lessons must be given to humanity in the language of humanity" (*The Desire of Ages*, p. 34). The more familiar you are with the Bible, the clearer it becomes that every part of God's Word was given in the time, place, language, and culture of specific human beings. Paul, with his "Ph.D.," expresses God's revelation in a different way than does Peter, the fisherman. John writes in simple, clear, almost childlike Greek. In contrast, the author of Hebrews writes in complex and literary Greek. In Matthew, you have someone who understands the Jewish mind and seeks to meet it. Mark, on the other hand, reaches out to the Gentile mind. The Greek language of the New Testament is quite different from the classical Greek of Plato and Aristotle—so much so that in the nineteenth century many scholars thought New Testament Greek was some sort of "heavenly language," different from any other form of ancient Greek. Then an expedition to Egypt was organized in 1895 with the express purpose of finding documents from the ancient world. Reports suggested that the town of Oxyrhynchus would be a good place to start.

In Oxyrhynchus, scholars stumbled upon a massive ancient garbage dump with numerous piles as high as thirty feet, including the rubbish of several centuries. When the scholars started digging into the piles of ancient trash, they found a treasure trove of ordinary documents from everyday life in New Testament times; these documents were well preserved because very little decomposition had taken place in the dry Egyptian climate. They found still more everyday documents in the ruins of houses;

others had been buried with their owners. Some discarded documents had even been used to make painted decorations on the wrappings of mummies, both human and animal. These documents included personal letters, wills, accounts, bills, receipts, and agreements regarding divorce, marriage, adoption, and land sales.

When scholars began studying these everyday documents of the ancient Mediterranean world, they made a shocking discovery. The language of these documents was not the scholarly Greek of Plato and Aristotle or the public Greek of law and government—it was the language of the Greek New Testament! The common people of the ancient world and the writers of the New Testament were using the same language—the everyday language of people on the street! The New Testament was not written in a heavenly language nor in the cultured language of the elite but in the everyday language of everyday people. *In the New Testament, God went out of His way to meet people where they were!*

One might argue that the everyday language of the New Testament is simply the inevitable result of the human authors God chose to use. They were just using the language they were familiar with, and God had nothing to do with it. But the scriptural evidence shows otherwise. In the book of Daniel God even adjusted the *content* of visions in order to more effectively communicate to His prophets. Let me demonstrate this from the text.

In Daniel 2 and Daniel 7 the same basic message was presented to two different "prophets"—Nebuchadnezzar and Daniel. God gave both men a vision of four consecutive kingdoms followed by a different kind of kingdom, followed by the kingdom of God (see Daniel 2:28; cf. Daniel 7:1). In each case the message of the vision was that God was in control of the affairs of human history. He is the One who sets up kings and puts them down (see Daniel 2:21), and His "Son of Man" would have dominion over the kingdoms of this world (see Daniel 7:13, 14, 27). The two messages were virtually the same in essential content.

But to the pagan king Nebuchadnezzar, God portrayed the future in terms of an idol, something Nebuchadnezzar could easily understand (see Daniel 2:29–36). It's clear from Daniel 3 that the image of Daniel 2 is an idol. Nebuchadnezzar knew exactly what to do with that image—set it up to be worshiped! This means of communication to Nebuchadnezzar makes perfect sense. To the king the great nations of the world were bright, shining examples of the gods they worshiped. God met Nebuchadnezzar where he was.

But to the Hebrew prophet Daniel, God portrayed the future in terms of the Creation story of Genesis 1 and 2 (see Daniel 7:2–14). The vision to Daniel begins with a stormy sea that has a wind blowing over it (see Daniel 7:2; cf. Genesis 1:2). Then animals begin to appear (see Daniel 7:3–6; cf. Genesis 2:19, 20). Then there is a "Son of Man" who is given dominion over the animals (see Daniel 7:13, 14; cf. Genesis 1:26, 28). This is a powerful recollection of the Adam story at Creation. God's message to Daniel was something like this: just as Adam had dominion over the animals at Creation, God's "Son of Man," when He comes, will have dominion over the nations that were hurting Daniel's people. In other words, God is still in control of history, even when things look completely out of control. God meets people where they are, and He certainly met Daniel and Nebuchadnezzar where they were.

This is also the reason we have four Gospels in the New Testament instead of just one. The fact that there are four Gospels in the Bible tells us that no one, not even an inspired writer, can reach everyone with the message about Jesus. We all see with limited vision. A variety of Gospels enables a variety of audiences to grasp the implications of Jesus' life and death for their own lives and experiences. Some people gravitate to the Gospel of Matthew; others prefer Luke or John. Telling the story of Jesus in a variety of ways meets a variety of people where they are. This seems to be the way God prefers to work.

The ultimate example of God meeting people where they are is the person of Jesus Himself. When God chose to reveal Himself in person, He did not come as "Jesus Christ Superstar." He became a first-century Jew, living in Palestine, who talked in terms appropriate to the local language and culture. He got dirty, hungry, and tired. At times, He even became frustrated, angry, and sad (see Mark 1:40, 41; 3:4, 5; 6:6; 10:13, 14). God didn't choose to send us a "superstar" but One just like ourselves. The incarnation of Jesus demonstrates the depth of God's commitment to meeting human beings where they are in their specific times, places, languages, and circumstances.

Ellen White clearly articulated this principle in *Selected Messages,* book 1, pages 19–22.

> The writers of the Bible had to express their ideas in human language. It was written by human men. These men were inspired of the Holy Spirit. . . .

The Scriptures were given to men, not in a continuous chain of unbroken utterances, but piece by piece through successive generations, as God in His providence saw *a fitting opportunity* to impress man at sundry times and divers places. . . .

The Bible is written by inspired men, but it is not God's mode of thought and expression. It is that of humanity. God, as a writer, is not represented. . . .

The Bible, perfect as it is in its simplicity, does not answer to the great ideas of God; for infinite ideas cannot be perfectly embodied in finite vehicles of thought.

This incarnational principle motivated Paul in his missionary endeavors. His clearest reflection on the matter (see 1 Corinthians 9:19–23) is a mandate for secular ministry. Paul tells us that it requires considerable sacrifice to reach out to people who are different from ourselves. If we have had little success sharing the gospel with secular people, it is because we haven't chosen to make that sacrifice:

> Though I am free from all men, I have made myself a servant to all, that I might win the more;
>
> and to the Jews I became as a Jew, that I might win Jews; to those who are under the law, as under the law, that I might win those who are under the law;
>
> to those who are without law, as without law (not being without law toward God, but under law toward Christ), that I might win those who are without law;
>
> to the weak I became as weak, that I might win the weak. I have become all things to all men, that I might by all means save some.
>
> Now this I do for the gospel's sake, that I may be partaker of it with you (1 Corinthians 9:19–23, NKJV).

In this passage, Paul gives a mandate for secular ministry. It is a mandate for reaching out to people who are different than we are; it is a mandate for learning how to speak to people in a language that makes sense to them where they are. And the bonus is that if we are willing to make the necessary sacrifices, there is an excellent likelihood that many more people will come to Christ than would otherwise do so!

"Lessons must be given to humanity in the language of humanity." People need to be addressed in a language with which they are familiar. The reason that the Adventist message is spreading like wildfire in places like New Guinea, the Philippines, Kenya, and parts of the Caribbean is that Adventism as we normally express it is exactly what those people are looking for. But in other places the same message seems out of context. God meets people where they are. And He invites us to follow His example and do the same.

## Human learning styles

A second reason we need to meet people where they are is because that is how people learn best. We used to think of people in terms of "smart" and "stupid." We assumed that some people are just plain smarter than others. But now we have come to realize that a lot of the differences in how people learn have to do with learning styles. Some people may appear unintelligent because the way material is presented to them doesn't fit their learning style. But when these same people are allowed to learn according to their unique learning style, it becomes evident that they are actually quite smart in their own way. Of course, most parents of multiple children knew this decades ago.

I have three children. When they were small, one of our favorite family activities was reading books together. I would pick out a children's book that told, for example, the story of a bunny rabbit hopping through the woods. I would sit down in my favorite easy chair, and the family would gather around on the couch or on the carpet near my chair.

But things never stayed quite so calm and organized. As I began reading the story, my oldest daughter would start repeating the story after me! I would read a sentence, and then she would interrupt and start retelling the sentence, sometimes in the same words and sometimes in her own words. Frankly, I found this rather irritating. I would tell her in no uncertain terms that *I* was the one telling the story—not she. Her job was to keep quiet and listen. And I thought I was being a good parent, training her in proper behavior so she would be successful in school! Maybe so, but I was completely blind to her learning style.

I have come to realize since then that my oldest daughter is an auditory learner. She learns best through what she hears. So, when she was repeating the story after me, she was reinforcing the content of the story in her own mind. She was learning in the way that worked best for her. Unfortunately, most schools (and at least one father, evidently) are not set up so that an auditory learner like her can be most successful. In school, children are expected to be quiet when the teacher is talking. That makes for efficiency and order but is not the best learning atmosphere for many students.

My son, on the other hand, seems to be more of a visual learner. Perhaps 60 percent of all learners pick up information primarily through what they see. So, when I started reading a story about the bunny rabbit hopping through the forest, Joel would get up, bound across the room, hop onto the arm of my chair (another no-no in our family), and grab the book out of my hands! What was he doing? He wanted to see the picture of the bunny hopping through the forest! Because he was a visual learner, the story meant more to him when combined with the pictures that could be seen only from the vantage point of my seat.

Again, I thought that this childish behavior called for some "training" in good learning etiquette. I ordered him back to where he came from and chided him for disrupting the story. And the average teacher in most schools would probably react in much the same way I did. You can't run a class of twenty students if everyone is running up to the teacher's desk at the same time to look at the same book! Yet, I now realize that my son was trying to learn in the way that works best for him. A story that he could experience through what he saw would be a story that he would never forget.

But the chaos didn't end with my son. You see, my youngest daughter is a kinetic learner. That means that she learns best when she is wiggling or moving around. So, when she heard the story of the bunny rabbit hopping through the forest, she would get up from her seat and start going *boing, boing, boing,* bouncing and hopping around the room. The story would have the greatest impact on her if she could act it out. She was learning in the way that worked best for her. Of course, I again took the opportunity to do some parental "training."

These different learning styles certainly make things challenging for teachers. Formal school has proven challenging for each of my children in different ways. Are they dumb? Absolutely not! Each of my children has demonstrated striking brilliance in one or more areas. But each of them learns best when they are free to apply their unique learning style to the educational situation.

The lesson in this for us is that the more we meet people where they are—intellectually, culturally, and in terms of their unique learning styles—the more success we will have in presenting the gospel to them. We need to meet people where they are, not only because God does it that way but because that is the way people learn best.

## Barriers against persuasion

A third reason to meet people where they are is that every human being has a built-in barrier against persuasion. James Engel, in the book *Contemporary Christian Communications,* discusses this at some length.* He notes that information processing is highly selective in human beings. In other words, we all tend to see and hear what we want to see and hear. People are fully capable of resisting attempts to influence them, and there is no magic potion that guarantees that the message you want to present will be taken seriously.

In today's world, everyone's attention is pulled in multiple directions. In order to cope with the challenge, we selectively withdraw from some options in order to place our attention on others. When you try to present the gospel to someone, you are competing against a wide variety of other options for that person's attention. Individuals rapidly classify incoming messages in terms of what will be useful or pertinent to their lives. People tend to give attention to messages that are relevant to their lives at that particular time. In other words, human beings have a "filtering system" that enables them to tune out messages that don't address the needs they feel at the moment. If they have little interest in the message, they will tune it out.

Related to this is a parallel discovery. Human beings have a natural aversion to changing their minds. They resist changes in strongly held beliefs and attitudes. And this aversion to change is good. If we didn't have it, we would all change religions every day. We would all believe the last thing we were told. People with a low aversion to changing their minds are known as credulous or easily duped. Most of us don't want to be like that, and most of us are not like that.

The average person has a strong barrier against persuasion. When somebody comes along with an idea that is radically different from what they

---

* (Nashville, Tenn.: Thomas Nelson, Inc., 1979), 47–57.

believe, what happens? A psychological brick wall goes up. And the more you pound against that wall, the more it is reinforced. Engel calls it a "God-given defense" against unwanted persuasion. If someone comes at you against the grain, you have the capacity to simply tune them out. Even the most powerful advertising does not cause people to act against their natural desires.

But there is a way around those "brick walls." There is a way around selective attention. And the way around is to approach people in the area of their felt needs. A felt need is a point in a person's life when what is being presented intersects with that person's own conscious needs and interests, where they are open to instruction. Students of world mission call this felt need the point of contact. It works with both individuals and groups. It is the point in a person's or a group's experience when they are open to instruction, when the gospel intersects with their perceived need.

I remember a time when I had a huge felt need. I was a young parent, and my biggest felt need had to do with "potty training." Some toddlers love that warm feeling in their pants! How do you get them to do what they are supposed to do in the place they're supposed to do it? No matter what I did, one particular child preferred to do things differently than I wanted. At that point I was wide open to information on the subject of "potty training," no matter how crazy the suggestion might sound! All a person had to do was say, "I had a kid just like that, and here's what worked for us." I gave that person my full and immediate attention. And no matter how nutty the idea sounded, my wife and I tried it at least once, because we felt a huge need to resolve that problem.

Around the same time someone came to me arguing that "President Ronald Wilson Reagan is the beast of Revelation because he has six letters in each of his three names." The idea made no sense to me then and makes even less sense to me now. And in any case, adopting that view would not make my life better. So, I frankly had no interest in that person's opinion. But when someone shared the idea of a "musical potty" (leave a deposit, get a song!), I was all ears. While the musical potty idea sounds crazy to me now, at the time my felt need made the idea worth investigating. My barrier against persuasion came down immediately. Secular people are no different. When you approach them at the point of a felt need, they are wide open to instruction.

In my book *Present Truth in the Real World,* I tell the story of a blood-pressure-screening ministry in New York City back in the 1970s. Only one out of every twenty or thirty people who had their blood pressure checked expressed an interest in Bible studies when asked. Then someone created Bible studies that helped people cope with the stress of life in the big city. As soon as these lessons were available, the number of people who accepted Bible studies skyrocketed to about five out of every six (about 85 percent). The moment they were told, "We have a free set of Bible study guides on how to cope with stress," people were just grabbing them, sometimes collecting extras for their friends. One day, in front of the New York Stock Exchange, 242 people came to have their blood pressure checked, and every single one accepted Bible studies! Two hundred forty-two out of two hundred forty-two! It must have been a *very* bad day on Wall Street! But that is what happens when you meet felt needs—the barrier against persuasion is gone. That's what meeting people where they are is all about.

Now, the leaders of the blood-pressure ministry in New York have always insisted that the key to their success was primarily the outpouring of the Holy Spirit in response to prayer. Ministry to secular people will succeed only in an atmosphere of God's presence and power. Nevertheless, attention to people's felt needs is a major corollary to the Spirit's work. Prayer without an understanding of method will work wonders. But even more powerful is a ministry that combines prayer with intelligent sensitivity to how secular people can be best approached.

Meeting people where they are does not make life easier for those who want to reach secular people. Secular people are as diverse as snowflakes. Talk to twenty of them, and you will likely discover twenty different sets of felt needs, many of which you will have never met in quite that form before. But meeting people where they are will prove to be a great adventure that will enrich your life. And we meet people where they are because that is what God does, because that is how people learn, and because it bypasses the God-given human barrier against persuasion. When our lives are also bathed in prayer, this is the basic formula for success.

Meeting people where they are means that analyzing the audience is the first step in reaching out to the secular mainstream, whether modern or postmodern. We need to listen before we talk. People have the power to tune out the gospel. If we fail to meet them where they are, the message will not reach them even if it is staring them in the face. We need to spend time discovering the felt needs of individuals and groups before the gospel can be presented to them in power.

## Illustrations

A couple of stories from the mission field are powerful examples of what happens when people follow—or don't follow—the principle of meeting people where they are. One of these stories took place in Irian Jaya, the western part of the island of New Guinea.* A missionary couple went upriver into the interior and settled in with the Sawi, a group of tree-dwellers who had had no previous contact with the outside world. The couple tried to understand the Sawi's language and customs. They ministered to their medical needs and brought them major advances in technology, such as mirrors, knives, and axes. Because of the advantages the couple brought to the tribe, the people welcomed them with great enthusiasm.

When the couple reached a working knowledge of the language, the husband felt it was time to try to present the gospel. He went to the longhouse and told the story of Jesus. And he did it well. But the Sawi showed little interest in the story of Jesus. They didn't much care what "the greatest Spirit" had done for some far-off tribe (the Jews) in a faraway land. The biblical message did not seem to apply to them until the missionary came to the story of how Judas betrayed Jesus. Suddenly, the people began cheering and celebrating. The missionary was mystified by their behavior until he discovered that, for them, the hero of the story was Judas, not Jesus!

Why? Because in their particular culture, the highest level of respect was reserved for what we would call treachery. The Sawi honored Judas as someone courageous enough to betray his best friend. They were impressed that he could keep close company for three years with a powerful figure like Jesus, sharing His food, traveling together, and finally betraying Him all by himself, without any of the other disciples ever suspecting! Such treachery exceeded all the examples they had honored through the years.

How does one present the gospel to people like that? The local culture honored and revered behavior that was directly contrary to the gospel. From the missionary couple's perspective, the husband's presentation of the gospel had been clear, powerful, and convincing. But to the Sawi tree-dwellers,

---

* See Don Richardson, *Peace Child* (n.p.: Regal Books, 1975).

the gospel story confirmed their own hideous practices. The gospel is not truly heard or understood until it comes to people in context. But where in that hideous culture was a context for the gospel?

Shortly after the couple's attempt to share the gospel, war broke out between the Sawi and another group the couple had been working with, as well. The couple did their best to intervene in the conflict but to no avail. Finally, in frustration, they told the people that they would leave and go to other tribes who would not betray and kill each other. Because the people didn't want to lose the economic benefits that the couple had brought, they promised to make peace. But how do you make peace in an environment that glorifies treachery?

Their treacherous culture did allow for an impressive and effective peace ceremony. Warriors from the two tribes faced each other in an open area. A leading man from each tribe, in anguish and trembling, selected one of his own treasured baby boys and brought him to the most trusted man on the other side. Each baby became known as the "peace child." Each tribe loved and guarded their peace child. The peace child was their protection from the other tribe. As long as that child lived, they knew that they would be safe from attack. Why? Because they had become "family." You could betray a friend, but you couldn't betray family. As long as the peace child lived, the two tribes would be at peace with one another.

The couple observed all that had happened and asked many questions. Here was the redemptive analogy they had been looking for! At their next opportunity to address the Sawi, they told about a war between heaven and earth. They told how God so loved the world that He sent a "Peace Child" to the human race. He gave His Son to the human "tribe." And although peace among the Sawi people lasted only as long as the peace child lived, God made *permanent* peace available in Jesus, because He now lives forever. God was now on their side. They had become family! This gospel in context appealed effectively to the Sawi, and many of the tree-dwellers accepted Christ.

A similar experience occurred in a part of the world far distant from New Guinea. Ed Dickerson tells the story of Bruce Olson's attempt to take the gospel to the Motilón people in a remote part of South America. Olson learned to speak the language, and the people came to accept his presence. Eventually, his closest Motilón friend became a Christian, but the work proceeded slowly.

One Motilón custom included marathon singing sessions in which, suspended in hammocks high above the ground, they sang out the news that each person had heard and experienced during the last few days. During one of these festivals, Olson listened as his friend, the first Motilón Christian, sang out the story of Jesus and the story of his personal conversion. For fourteen hours, while a formerly hostile neighboring chief repeated it word for word and note for note, the gospel rang out through the jungle night.

Although this was a positive development, the missionary himself was uncomfortable with what happened. "It seemed so heathen," he wrote. "The music, chanted in a strange minor key, sounded like witch music. It seemed to degrade the gospel. Yet, when I looked at the people around me and up at the chief, swinging in his hammock, I could see they were listening as though their lives depended upon it. Bobby was giving them spiritual truth through the song."

The music sounded like "witch music" to the missionary. It was Motilón music. Yes, their music, as well as their language, had previously served false gods. Yet, the missionary would not hesitate to translate the Bible into the Motilón language in spite of its pagan connotations. The gospel had to come to the Motilón people in a language they could understand.

The same was true of their music. How could God sing to the Motilón except in a musical language that communicated to them? Bach chorales and early American folk hymns wouldn't do the job. The missionary's Laodicean comfort zone had become an obstacle to presenting the gospel. When it came to spiritual things, he thought his way was the only right way, his favorite Christian music the only appropriate music for communicating the gospel. He seemed unable to move past his comfort zone, so God bypassed him and sang to the Motilón in their own way.*

The challenge to communication in both these stories occurs on a smaller scale every day and all around the globe. People struggle to find the right words to communicate what they are thinking. Communication is a struggle because every person on earth has what I call a "cultural horizon." Every person has areas of specialty and areas of limitation. Let me illustrate this concept from the physical world.

---

* Ed Dickerson, "Dead Languages," *Adventist Review*, March 4, 2004, 28; based on Bruce Olson, *Bruchko* (Orlando, Fla.: Creation House, 1973), 146.

In a room, each person's physical horizon is the four walls and the ceiling of the room, with a bit of a view out the windows. If I go outside, my horizon expands, but it may still be limited. In a city, for example, the horizon is limited by buildings and landscaping. In a valley, the horizon is limited by the trees and hills. In flat, treeless country, one can see even farther. But if you can get on top of a mountain peak, your horizon expands much farther still.

Every human being also has a cultural horizon. This is a horizon of the intellect, of the emotions, of experience. Our knowledge and experience tend to be limited by such factors as our geography, family background, and schooling. When we encounter another human being, we can communicate most effectively at the points of common interests and common understandings. Education is the intellectual equivalent of climbing a mountain. That is its chief value. The more education you receive, the broader your horizon and the greater your potential for influence on others in this world. You become able to communicate particular thoughts in a variety of forms and expressions. What counts is not the particular form you choose but whether the hearer clearly understands your intended meaning.

A major purpose of this book is to broaden the reader's horizon to include an understanding of the cultural horizon or worldview of secular people. In dealing with the secular environment, Adventists face a problem similar to that of the missionary couple in New Guinea. In interacting with secular people, we often encounter ideas so distinct from ours that there is little or no meaningful interaction. What must take place at such times in order for communication to happen? At least one of the two individuals seeking to communicate must broaden his horizon to include the other.

Whose responsibility should it be to broaden horizons in a witnessing context? "Lessons must be given to humanity in the language of humanity," Ellen White wrote. If this statement is true, some Adventists, at least, need to learn how to speak to secular people. Who are secular people? What will it take to reach them? In the last decade, things have become even more complicated. There are now two distinct forms of secularism in today's world. What works with one type of secular person may not work with the other.

# CHAPTER TWO

# New Developments Require New Definitions

## The basic concept

What do we mean by secular people? Here's a brief, but practical, definition: *A secular person is someone who lives from day to day with little or no reference to God or the practices of formal religion.* Most secular people are not atheists and have not made a conscious decision to be a "secular person." They may well believe in God, but for them, involving God or religion in their everyday decisions and actions is not a priority. The typical secular person may not be hostile to religion, but he or she does not seek out or enjoy many traditional practices of religion, such as prayer, attending worship services, or reading the Bible.

Secularism is more obvious in places like North America, Europe, and Australia, but it is increasingly present in all parts of the globe that are open to mass communication. The influence of television, movies, music, magazines, and the Internet has promoted secular thinking and practice in some surprising places. For example, one of my African students expressed little interest in this subject of secularism; he considered it a Western problem. But six months after he returned to Africa, he wrote me a letter saying, "When I got back to my country with a master's degree, they made me the pastor of the church in the capital city. I found out I have twenty-six Ph.D.s in my church, and all the secular influences you talked about are happening right here."

I have made a number of trips to Africa since hearing that report. While there are certainly traditional villages that seem to have little awareness of the wider world, most Africans are just as eager to enter the wider world as people anywhere else. So, although this book, like its predecessor, is written largely with the Western situation in mind, its concepts and principles will prove relevant to nearly every part of the globe. The resurgence of militant Islam and the expansion of the charismatic movement among Christians may seem to be diminishing secularism's impact. However, there are still large numbers of people in nearly every country who resist the inroads of religion in their lives. They may conform to the outward trappings of religion, but their hearts are increasingly tied to the "religion" of consumerism and worldly success.

## Two types of secular people

In my book *Present Truth in the Real World* I treated the phenomenon of secular people as a single entity. While secular people were, and are, diverse in their individualism, secularism had a number of common characteristics one could almost always count on. That has now changed. Spirituality and faith are much more a part of everyday consciousness than they were ten years ago, especially in the media. People are more comfortable talking casually about their spiritual commitments. I find this to be true in Adventist congregations and educational centers, as well. Many people both inside and outside of the church are hungry to touch the substance behind the doctrines, institutions, and forms in which faith has been expressed. This hunger was not nearly so obvious ten years ago.

At the same time, however, Christian churches have not found their challenges diminishing. Faith and spirituality may be held in higher esteem today than in the past, but religion, in general, is not. As commonly understood, faith and spirituality have made a certain peace with secular thinking so that faith and secularism can exist side by side without bothering anyone. But strong convictions remain suspect. Criticism of other faiths is considered out of line. People are leaving "denominations" to join independent, spiritual movements.

I have learned in the last few years that "secular people" now come in two fairly distinct forms that have some core similarities but are quite different in other areas. Understanding the distinction between the two types of secular people is basic to understanding how to reach both varieties.

## Traditional secular people

The traditional secular person is someone who lives life without reference to God, whether or not he or she is conscious of doing so. Such individuals may well believe in God, yet they don't involve Him in the practical matters of everyday life. They don't normally pray before meals, they don't watch religious programming on television, and they rarely read the Bible or other religious literature. They may believe in God, but only a minority attend church on a regular basis. For them, the personal and corporate practices of religion simply have become irrelevant at the level of everyday experience.

Traditional secularism has been categorized in terms of four broad perspectives. Langdon Gilkey first presented these four perspectives in his book *Naming the Whirlwind,** and Tony Campolo later popularized them in the book *A Reasonable Faith.*† This four-part summary is helpful, but the average secular person on the street is not usually even conscious of these perspectives. We should also keep in mind that these are general patterns and that secular people don't think exactly alike.

*1. Contingency or Naturalism.* The word *contingency* describes the belief that everything in this world happens by natural cause and effect. Nothing is to be attributed to divine intervention. For example, if I am a bitter person, it is because of the way my parents raised me. If I am rich, it is because my parents were rich or because I worked hard. If I got an exceptionally good deal on a house or a car, it is not because God favors me; it is just the product of luck or my own skillful approach to business.

Another term for this way of thinking would be "naturalism." *Naturalism* means to live without the expectation of supernatural intervention. God is not at the edges of my life, seeking to benefit or harm me. That kind of thinking is considered superstitious. Instead, secular people live out their lives within the boundaries of reality as their five senses experience it. They are naturally skeptical about claims of supernatural intervention or miracles.

*2. Autonomy.* The second major aspect of secular thinking is called "autonomy." The word *autonomy* comes from the Greek language. It means a

---

* (Indianapolis: Bobbs-Merrill Company, 1969).
† (La Vergne, Tenn.: Lightning Source, 1995).

"law unto yourself." If God is not a living presence in everyday life, then people must take charge of their own lives. They must set their own rules.

Autonomous people sense little or no need for God's direction. It is up to me to decide how my life will be lived. It is up to me to determine what meaning my life will have. Meaning does not come down from heaven; neither do the answers to my questions or the solutions to my problems. Secular people live as if they were completely on their own in this world. They feel it is up to them to make the kinds of decisions that used to be left up to God.

*3. Relativity.* Closely related to "autonomy" is the concept of "relativity," the third basic aspect of the secular mind-set. If there is no supernatural intervention in everyday life and if human beings basically decide their own destiny, then meaning, values, and truth depend on the situation. What is right for one person might be wrong for another person. Homosexuality could be wrong for one generation yet acceptable for the next. Sex between consenting adults is fine as long as no one is overly shackled by guilt or shame as the result of some quaint notion of morality. If something is useful or if enough people practice it, it can be allowed or even encouraged. There is no external standard of morality. The community decides what is right or wrong.

*4. Temporality.* The fourth and final principle of secular thought and behavior is called "temporality." Temporality is the concept that this life is all there is. We arrive on this earth, we live for a short time, then we pass on. There is no lasting significance to anything we do; there are no rewards or punishments after the close of earthly consciousness. Since this life is all we can be sure of, it is advisable to live it with all the gusto you can. This concept was strikingly expressed in an athletic shoe commercial on television, "Life is short. Play hard." All that really matters is today. Tomorrow will have to take care of itself.

Taken together, these four perspectives of secularism—contingency (naturalism), autonomy, relativity, and temporality—make up a worldview dominated by the five senses. For the traditional secular person, reality is limited, at least in practical terms, to whatever human beings can tangibly experience, to what they can see, hear, touch, taste, or smell. For the secular person, the supernatural cannot be perceived by the five senses and is, therefore, irrelevant to life as we experience it.

Since people normally cannot see, hear, or touch God, the concept of a relationship with Him doesn't make sense to truly secular people. When unusual circumstances occur, the traditional secularist doesn't tend to see such events as God's actions. Instead, they assume that unusual events have a cause that would be scientifically explainable if we knew more about it. They see miracles as the products of ignorance rather than of faith. Science, since it operates on the basis of the five senses, is their primary authority in the area of knowledge.

We can see how dependent our world today is on the scientific method—how much its presuppositions are taken for granted—when we consider the fact that Martin Luther felt compelled to write a tract condemning Copernicus's radical view that the sun, rather than the earth, is the center of the solar system. Luther opposed Copernicus because he felt that the new astronomy was out of harmony with Scripture. Today, in spite of our respect for Luther, no Adventist I know would argue that Luther was correct. Clearly, science has opened our eyes to reality in ways that Luther did not expect. But the blessings of science have their dark side for faith. When, in practice, a person's view of truth is limited to the reality of the five senses, God is crowded out of that person's existence. Intuition and spiritual perception are seen as the products of wishful thinking.

Surprisingly, the traditional secular person is often quite "religious" in the sense that he or she will often be involved in a church of some sort. They may not know why they go. It may just be to please a spouse or parents. It may simply be because they have always gone to church. Yet, their spiritual life does not affect the core of their being. They go through the motions of religion, but they are not truly committed to them. A secular Adventist, for example, will do some things differently on the Sabbath, but the conversation is not likely to be guarded, and there is little conscious reference to God.

For genuine Christians, however, the totality of truth is bigger than the reality of our physical senses. Christians believe that beyond what our five senses are capable of experiencing is a wider reality that is equally true but not usually detectible through the physical senses. Here is where things get interesting. There is a new form of secularism that is open to the possibility of the supernatural and of life after death. This would seem to be a positive breakthrough for Adventist outreach. But this "postmodern" form of secularism, which we will now examine, still accepts the secular principles of autonomy and relativity, and it develops new wrinkles that are even more problematic for traditional expressions of Adventism.

## Postmodern secular people

Over the last ten to fifteen years, the concept of secularism has taken an interesting turn. These changes are related to what many have called "postmodernism," a phrase that seems to have arisen in the context of new forms of architecture. In many ways, today's younger generation, often called "postmoderns," are the polar opposites of traditional secular people. Where traditional secular people live life without significant reference to God, postmodern secular people tend to be very spiritual.

Postmodern secular people may spend significant amounts of time in personal, private prayer. They tend to enjoy the experience of worship, especially when it includes elements of contemporary music and style. They enjoy reading books about God and learning from people whose faith journey is radically different from their own. They like the informal fellowship of small groups as long as they are not bound to a long-term commitment. In other words, postmodern secular people will often seek and maintain a living relationship with God. Spirituality is a crucial component of their lifestyle.

In what sense, then, is the term *secular* appropriate to such spiritual people? What makes them "secular" is a strong aversion to the forms and institutions of religion. They may have a relationship with God, but they are not interested in having a relationship with institutional religions! They have strongly adopted two of the four characteristics of traditional secularism—autonomy and relativity. They believe in God and seek a relationship with Him, but they are not generally interested in externally imposed rules and moral mandates. They prefer to be in charge of their own spiritual journey.

Postmoderns, therefore, have a strong streak of "antiauthority" in their makeup. They are opposed to the authority of religious institutions. They feel that such institutions use lies and fantasies to control large numbers of gullible people and to get them to cough up money to keep the institution operating, whether or not the spiritual needs of the people are truly served. Postmoderns are interested in truth and interested in faith, but they are determined not to be subject to the faith claims of others. They may rejoice in God-talk with others but be quite resentful at attempts to proselytize. Some have come to call this attitude "postdenominationalism." We will have much more to say about the strengths and weaknesses of these postmodern, secular trends in future chapters.

From an Adventist perspective, postmodern secularism is, at first glance, an advance on the modernistic, scientific variety of secularism. It is much easier to talk to postmoderns about faith and values. But Adventist churches and other religious institutions are finding it harder and harder to harness these expressions of faith by postmodern secularists into a consistent and effective community. Postmoderns want to believe in God and serve their fellow humans, but they are suspicious of any attempts to organize groups that hold those beliefs. As a result, postmodernism, in spite of its spirituality and its affirmations of faith, is deeply challenging to the goals of Adventism or to those of any other traditional form of institutional religion.

## Conclusion

Whether we think of secular people in traditional or postmodern terms, we should avoid the assumption that secular people can be easily classified. The distinction between the two types of secular people is important and helpful. But there is no sharp dichotomy here. There are people who fit neatly into each category, but there are others who exhibit elements of both or who are in transition from traditional secular thinking to a more postmodern approach.

Secular people of both types can be as diverse as snowflakes even though there are some common patterns in the way they think. That diversity, of course, is the inevitable consequence of relativity. If there is no absolute standard for people's lives, there will be great diversity of belief and lifestyle among secular people.

The bottom line for Adventists is this: If we are serious about reaching the entire world with the gospel, we have to take these secular trends into account. Business as usual is no longer an option.

# CHAPTER THREE

# The Church in the Secular Environment

In many parts of the world, the secular environment is truly challenging to the Adventist faith. Great amounts of evangelistic effort yield increasingly limited results in comparison to the successes of the past. Increasingly, we seem to be talking over people's heads rather than making sense. These realities began to strike home for me when I pastored in New York City some thirty years ago.

At the time, Adventist membership in New York was approximately twenty thousand. Of that number less than three hundred members were white, English-speaking people (I am speaking of the five counties that make up the political core of New York City, not the whole metropolitan region). This reality was not due to any lack of white, English-speaking people in the city; there were several million, in fact. But they seemed uniquely resistant to Adventist attempts to interest them in the gospel message.

In 1980, for example, I held meetings three or four nights a week for virtually the whole year. I was targeting white males in particular and was thrilled to baptize about twelve relatively secular people with God's help. Then I phoned a friend who was a pastor in a neighboring church in the Northeastern Conference that specializes in ministry to African Americans. I had helped him that summer with a three-week tent campaign that resulted in the baptism of eighty-three people. When he found out that I had worked all year to baptize just twelve, he jokingly said, "What's wrong with you?"

Was something wrong with me? Perhaps not. After all, I had successfully helped him with his tent campaign. But there definitely seemed to be some sort of racial barrier that prevented people of European descent from appreciating the gospel. It was certainly tempting to suspect that European Americans might be more naturally resistant to the gospel than other people. Yet, that had not always been the case. Certainly when my German parents arrived in New York City in the 1930s, they found thriving German-speaking churches with nearly a thousand members. So, what was the real problem?

I began to share with my friend how secular thinking affected various groups of people, how it seemed to make people less receptive to the gospel. Suddenly, it became really quiet at the other end of the line.

He said, "I just realized something."

"What's that?" I asked.

"I just realized that we baptized eighty-three people, and not a single one is an American."

I said, "You see, you're beginning to face the same problems in your community. It's just easier to ignore the problem as long as you still have some receptive groups joining the church."

As a result of this conversation, I began to realize something. It doesn't matter if a person is black, Hispanic, or Asian; after a generation or two in New York City, having a decent income and a nice home in the suburbs, he or she is as impervious to the gospel as anyone of European descent. This observation was underlined by a study of Hispanic evangelism in Southern California. There, the Hispanic element of the Adventist Church grew explosively for several decades. So, a study was done to discover if the methods they used might be useful for other groups in the church.

The study, however, failed to isolate some approach that would work universally for all groups of people. Instead, the researchers discovered that immigration was the key element in the Hispanic growth in Southern California during those decades. Over a twenty-year period, not a single third- or fourth-generation Hispanic was baptized, who was not already married to an Adventist or who had some other connection with the church. Basically, the Hispanic Adventist church in Southern California was baptizing only immigrants and the children of immigrants. So, even in the most receptive sectors of society, the Adventist impact has been surprisingly limited.

An evangelistic innovation that has produced some success has been the Revelation Seminars. But even here the results have been mixed. For example, I remember a massive attempt to reach large numbers of people in a suburb of a major city. The suburb had a population of about sixty thousand and an average income well above the average. It was a typical upscale suburban neighborhood. More than a hundred thousand dollars was spent on advertising to that community, and forty pastors were brought in to hold Revelation Seminars on nearly every block! The result? A combined total of eight people showed up the first night! What on earth went wrong there?

The people in charge of the meetings contacted researchers at the Andrews University Seventh-day Adventist Theological Seminary in an attempt to figure out what had gone wrong. The Seminary, in turn, contacted the Donnelly Marketing Corporation in New York City, one of the "big five" Madison Avenue advertising agencies, for assistance. Donnelly representatives explained to Seminary personnel that there are forty-seven socioeconomic groups in North America. From the richest of the rich to the poorest of the poor, everyone in the United States and Canada belongs to one of these forty-seven groups. Once an ad executive knows which of these groups you belong to, he can tell you what kind of car you drive, what kind of toothpaste you use, even the foods that you prefer for breakfast. The reality is that we are all a bit more predictable than we think.

Donnelly analysts made a careful study of the kinds of people that attend evangelistic meetings and eventually join the Adventist Church. They correlated this information with their basic analytical grid of socioeconomic groups and made a rather stunning discovery. Among the forty-seven socioeconomic groups in North America, only four or five Anglo clusters respond to Revelation Seminars. In addition, another five to seven minority clusters also tend to respond positively to Revelation Seminars. When the Donnelly people correlated that information with the sixty-thousand people in the particular suburban community where the church had tried to hold Revelation Seminars, *only twelve individuals* fit into one of those four or five receptive groups! In other words, the Revelation Seminars had been extremely successful! Eight out of the twelve people who could reasonably be expected to respond actually showed up! That is a tremendous response to advertising! (Maybe the other four people were on vacation during that time.)

My purpose here is not to criticize traditional methods of evangelism. Most of them have functioned as long as they have because of their effectiveness. In different settings, with different demographics, Revelation Seminars draw a lot more people. Methods that are working with a given target audience should not be abandoned in the process of targeting other audiences.

But this experience illustrates the fact that the gospel needs to come to people in context. What works in one place may not work in another. We need to be aware of the unique needs and concerns of our audience. This principle is certainly in play when it comes to working with secular people.

Shortly after the events of September 11, Don Schneider, the new president of the North American Division and the same Don Schneider I had met in Colorado fifteen years earlier, visited the Adventist Theological Seminary with a proposal. He felt a burden to do something special for New York City in the wake of the terrorist attacks. He reported that things had changed dramatically in New York City. People were making eye contact on the street and in the subways. Secular people were showing an interest in spiritual things. People were coming to prayer meetings and attending church in record numbers.

So, Elder Schneider proposed (as he did to many other church entities) that the Seminary send one or two individuals to New York for a period of six months. Each individual would continue on salary and live in a high-rise apartment (the kind you can't enter unless you live there or know someone who does). The goal would be to get acquainted with the residents in the building and plant gospel seeds. The hope was that after six months there would be at least one Seventh-day Adventist in each building to carry on the mission.

Andrews University responded with enthusiasm. I led a Seminary fact-finding team to New York City in late October of 2001. We went fully prepared to discover that things had changed dramatically and that secular New Yorkers were now open to the gospel in ways that they hadn't been before. But by late October it was already clear that the dramatic spiritual changes that took place after September 11 had quickly faded due to the ongoing complexity of life in the big city.

Not willing to give up easily, however, Mark Regazzi from the undergraduate religion department went to midtown Manhattan for more than two months, and Don James from the Seminary went to Roosevelt Island (a small residential island a few hundred meters from midtown Manhattan) for nearly five months. Both individuals had a life-changing experience and made many wonderful contacts, but not one indigenous, secular New Yorker reached a point of serious interest in the Adventist message.

Our fact-finding team was not surprised. As part of our tour of New York City, we had visited a number of "cutting-edge" churches that were trying to reach out to mainstream New Yorkers. These churches were attracting people by the thousands. At the close of each service the individuals in our group fanned out among the attendees and interviewed as many as possible. We discovered that, as successful as these churches were in attracting large numbers of people, they were reaching few, if any, *secular* people. Most of the attendees had grown up as members of their respective denominations, drifted away, and then found themselves reattracted by an "accepting church." Not one person could realistically be called unchurched or secular, nor were they indigenous New Yorkers as a rule. Underlining the point, we learned that most Adventists attending churches in Manhattan (the center of the city) were immigrants who commuted to church from residences on the outskirts of the city.

We went home convinced that the observations I had made and the strategies I had drawn up in *Present Truth in the Real World* were still valid. Even in the wake of September 11, secular people were not normally reached by programs, strategies, or high-tech extravaganzas. They were not reached by religious media or jargon. They remained highly resistant to what most of us call "church." The level of spirituality among secular people may seem to have increased with the rise of "postmodernism," but that spirituality is not translating into large numbers of unchurched people joining traditional churches.

In the fall of 2002 I was picked up at London's Heathrow Airport by an officer of the British Union of Seventh-day Adventists. I had come to Britain to explore how the Adventist Church could more effectively engage the majority culture there with the Adventist message. I asked my driver to describe the situation in the British Union. He told me that while Great Britain had experienced massive immigration over the last twenty years, 95 percent of the general population was still English-speaking whites. But only about two thousand of the twenty thousand Adventists in the country represented the majority culture. On the other hand, although only 2 percent of the general population was of West Indian origin, 85 percent of the Adventist Church in Britain was from the West Indies. So, the Adventist Church in Britain looks and feels a lot different than the majority culture. In fact, only one hundred of the eight thousand Adventist members in London belonged to the majority culture at that time.

My first reaction was, "Thank God for the West Indians, or there wouldn't be an Adventist Church in Great Britain!" But it soon became clear that most Adventist Brits felt that the statistics indicated some sort of racial problem. They felt that blacks were naturally open to the gospel in Britain and that whites were naturally closed. And that was all there was to say about it.

Based on my experience in New York City and some earlier research, I suggested a different explanation. In North America, the divide of spiritual interest lies not between white and black but between indigenous and immigrant. Recent immigrants to North America from Eastern Europe have been wide open to the Adventist message, just as my German forebears had once been. But second- and third-generation German Americans are not being reached. Large numbers of blacks from places like Haiti, Jamaica, and Trinidad are baptized every year in New York City, yet the leadership of the Northeastern Conference is not aware of a single church that is successfully reaching African Americans (indigenous blacks). The famed Ephesus Seventh-day Adventist Church in Harlem is 95 percent immigrants as well as 80 percent commuters, indicating that, in spite of all the churches that can be found in Harlem, the neighborhood itself may increasingly house an unreached people group.

Church growth among immigrant Hispanics remains massive, yet we rarely baptize a third- or fourth-generation Hispanic. And finally, there are massive defections in the Asian community among second- and third-generation Korean Americans. This leads me to the conclusion that the real evangelistic challenge facing the Adventist Church in the Western world is not how to reach whites but how to reach the indigenous, secular, mainstream cultures of North America, Europe, Australia, and other developed countries such as Singapore. Although whites make up less than 1 percent of the population in Singapore, the Adventist Church there faces similar problems to those facing the church in the United States and Britain. So, when it comes to evangelism in Western countries, we are not facing a racial problem; we are facing an indigenous problem.

Before I continue, I want to be clear about one thing. When I say we are not facing a racial problem, I am speaking only about evangelism. I am not in any way, shape, or form suggesting that there are no issues of race in the Adventist Church. Racism remains among us in overt as well as covert forms. What I am highlighting here is the systematic neglect in Adventist evangelism of the African American and Chicano (indigenous Hispanic) communities. It is easy to think that if large numbers of dark-skinned and Spanish-speaking people are joining the church, we are doing fine among those people groups. But reality points to unreached people groups that are disguised among us. It is easy to "skim off" the hot interests, totally unaware that large segments of the audience aren't even listening.

When it comes to evangelism, therefore, we are not facing a racial problem but an indigenous problem. Nowhere in the developed world—and certainly not in the Islamic world, either—are we reaching the mainstream culture. In such areas, our baptisms are limited largely to recent arrivals.

When I shared these thoughts with the mostly West Indian audience of Adventist pastors in south England, one pastor asked, "Why are we wasting time talking about hard-to-reach people? We don't have time for this. Let's invest our time and money on people groups that are open. If the majority culture isn't open to the gospel, it's not our problem."

His comments certainly reflected the feeling of many West Indian pastors and people in Great Britain. The approach he suggested, however, is not realistic for the long term.

I responded, "Do you care if your children and grandchildren are in the church? My experience as a second-generation German American tells me that your children and grandchildren will be indigenous Brits; they won't be West Indians anymore. If the church doesn't learn how to reach indigenous Brits, it won't interest your children and grandchildren either."

Now my audience was ready for battle! A white pastor spoke up, "There's something here I don't understand. When the Adventist Church first came to Great Britain toward the end of the nineteenth century, it reached the British mainstream. If that wasn't so, we wouldn't have any Anglos in the church at all right now. What has changed between then and now?"

This question was one of those magical moments for me. Suddenly a whole lot of things came into perspective that I had never connected before. For just a moment I caught a glimpse of the mighty hand of God in the last place I would have looked. My experience in Great Britain was the key to my new perspective, but I believe it is even more relevant to the situation in North America.

What I shared briefly in response to this white pastor's question I will share in more detail in the next chapter. It unpacks how I think God has brought us to the place where we are today. It shows us why Adventism was once so effective in the Western world and why it is struggling today. For me, the next chapter changes everything.

# CHAPTER FOUR

# How People Approach Truth

Every few hundred years the world goes through a massive transformation, something we have come to call a "paradigm shift." In a matter of decades society seems to totally rearrange itself. Worldviews change, social and political structures are transformed, the things people value aren't the same as those valued by a previous generation. The way people determine what is true about their world is altered. From one generation to the next, society enters an entirely new world. The people born into that world cannot even imagine what the world of their grandparents must have been like. They have a hard enough time understanding their parents.

We are currently experiencing such a paradigm shift. It is the change from modernism to postmodernism. In fact, some sociologists feel that the change has just begun, and the ultimate shape of the postmodern world is yet to be fully grasped. Postmodernism is not yet an organized worldview or culture. But already we know enough to begin assessing the impact of these changes on the church and its mission. Perhaps the best way to start is to review previous transformations over the last thousand years or so.

While a "short history of religious thought" risks superficiality, in this case it provides us with a basic handle on the major changes that shape today's world. During the last decade or so, the gospel has begun encountering an entirely new context. The basic question that will guide us in this survey of religious thought can be expressed in the following way: "How do people decide what is true and what is not true? How do they determine truth?" The answer has undergone a number of changes over the last five hundred years.

## The premodern period

In the Middle Ages (the premodern period) truth was thought to reside in privileged groups. In other words, the average person on the street didn't try to figure out what was true or what was not true. Ordinary people didn't have a clue and didn't expect to. They believed truth could be found only in the clergy or in the church. So, if a medieval person wanted to know the truth, they went and talked to a priest. They accepted whatever the priest said as the way things really were.

People were not used to questioning what the church taught. In fact, in the Crusades individuals were willing to kill and to die for "the truth" as the clergy had declared it to them. You could say that the leaders of the church had "privileged" access to the truth. It was God's will that the leaders He ordained would have the truth and pass it on to the people as needed.

Likewise, in the political realm there was the sense that kings and nobles knew best how the nation ought to be run. The average person didn't involve himself or herself in such matters. Theirs was not to reason why; theirs was but to do and die.

But what if a person in the Middle Ages went to two or more priests and got differing answers to his question? This was a very likely occurrence. What happened then? Not to worry. A system was in place to handle this kind of confusion. Whenever the priests would disagree, a bishop would decide the truth. And if a bishop couldn't decide or if the bishops disagreed with each other, the pope or a decision of one of the "great councils" would decide the matter. That way, the perception of truth could be controlled, and the people didn't need to be confused about such matters. In all of this, the important point is that in medieval times the conduit of truth ran through privileged people groups; namely, the church and its representatives. Truth was an idea reserved for those who were "in the know."

Western society as a whole has moved far beyond premodernism, yet you will still find individuals who settle the issue of truth in a similar way. Many people—among them Seventh-day Adventists—still demonstrate a high degree of submission to whatever the pastor, the priest, the rabbi, or the imam says is true. This is even more the case in those developing countries where medieval-style cultures still hold sway, especially in the rural areas. In such contexts, this way of determining truth goes beyond the field of religion and may include civil leaders such as the local chiefs of that people group. But under the influence of the media, most cultures in the developing world are moving toward a more participatory way of determining what is true for that local group. And in those cultures leadership is usually quite stressed about the loss of support and confidence among the people.

## Christian modernism

With the Reformation, people's confidence in privileged people and groups began to break down. Truth was no longer seen to reside primarily in the church or the state but rather in logical statements based on careful biblical research. People came to think that priests, popes, and nobles had no greater access to truth than anyone else. They came to view the Bible—not churches or bishops—as the ultimate source and safeguard for truth. The search for truth was an act of reason and logic; with diligence and talent, anyone could understand the truth for himself through careful study of the Scriptures. I call this approach to truth "Christian modernism."

The search for truth, therefore, became more of an individual pursuit than one carried out by privileged groups such as church leadership. People took more personal responsibility for what they believed. The search for truth involved individual researchers carefully examining the Bible and then sharing what they found. If others were convinced by their arguments, movements would form around various teachers' perceptions of the Bible. The inherent individualism of the process, however, tended to produce fragmentation. The Reformation resulted in many denominations, each seeking to be faithful to the biblical vision of its founder or founders.

The Christian modernism worldview dominated nineteenth-century America. Its rugged individualism and appreciation for logical rigor were at the core of the American Revolution and its democratic ideals. Christian modernism was also the setting in which Adventism got its start and upon which Adventism based its logical appeal to the American mainstream. The Adventist pioneers were rugged individualists who searched the Scriptures with rigor and intensity. They argued their cases with each other, and the movement might well have fragmented (like the first-day

Adventist groups) had it not been for the unifying guidance of Ellen White's prophetic gift. Since the teachings of Adventism were so grounded in the biblical logic and worldview of nineteenth-century America, the Adventist presentation of truth had compelling power.

The same is true in a wider sense today. Anywhere in the world that the Christian modernism viewpoint dominates, Adventism still reaches the mainstream of society with power. When the Adventist message first arrived in Great Britain, toward the end of the nineteenth century, the mainstream culture of Britain was still Christian modern. So, the Adventist message was quite attractive to indigenous Brits, and many thousands of people joined the church. Similarly, the traditional tools of Adventist evangelism are still effective in many places today. But the number of such areas is shrinking rapidly. The spearhead of philosophical change has already moved two generations past that of nineteenth-century America. Great Britain, for example, is no longer a Christian modern culture, and Adventism struggles to reach the mainstream there. This is generally true throughout the Western world and increasingly elsewhere. In fact, the philosophical changes in society have been far greater in the last hundred years than in the previous two thousand years combined. And it is these changes that are the focus of the rest of this book.

## Secular modernism

Beginning with the so-called Enlightenment in eighteenth-century Europe, the world experienced a shift away from Christian modernism to secular modernism. Philosophers and other intellectuals were already making this move in the eighteenth century, but it wasn't until the early decades of the twentieth century that secular modernism became the dominant worldview in North America. The fundamentalist-liberal controversy of the 1920s provided something of a rite of passage in which conservative Christianity (in its Christian modernist form) lost touch with the mainstream of American society.

One of the main goals of the Enlightenment was to eliminate superstition by exposing the flaws in all previous thinking. The key to truth was methodological doubt. Descartes, for one, doubted everything until he could demonstrate its truthfulness in a logical and compelling way. He would, no doubt, have agreed with the words of Ellen White: "We have many lessons to learn and many, many to unlearn" (*The Review and Herald*,

July 26, 1892). As flawed thinking was increasingly exposed, the end result would be a "bombproof" residue of truth in which one could have absolute confidence. With continued application of the scientific method, these "assured results" could be gradually increased until life could be lived with a fair amount of confidence that we knew what was going on.

Another foundation of secular modernism was advancement in the physical sciences. Scientists such as Isaac Newton found the universe to be a very orderly place, subject to laws that could be tested and confirmed. The "truths" of physical science were verifiable. So truth, in a very practical sense, seemed within reach if the right approach were taken. From the motion of the stars down to the tiniest atom, everything seemed to operate in an observable and consistent fashion. The modernist believed, therefore, that through a careful scientific approach it would be possible to attain intellectual certainty about many things.

The practical outcome of scientific knowledge is power over nature. By understanding nature, human beings can control it and use it for their own purposes. Knowledge is power, and the technologies based on that knowledge began to improve the condition of human beings. And because science so clearly worked in the practical realm (for example, it enabled airplanes to fly), people began to trust it even in the spiritual realm.

Secular modernists, therefore, came to believe that truth could be found by applying careful, scientific method to all questions, even religious questions. Truth was not to be found in the church or in the Bible; rather, it was to be found in a scientific process of careful observation and experimentation. The core of this scientific process is a reliance on the five senses. The only reliable source of truth is what human beings can see, hear, touch, taste, or smell. Feelings are not to be trusted. Truth is found by the application of reason. Misperceptions are always possible, of course, but a rigorous scientific process ensures that reality is properly observed and understood. Science, therefore, not only became a window into the physical world; modernists came to believe it could also be the source of truth in the spiritual world.

Because of its trust in science, however, modernity lost interest in the supernatural, which was not subject to scientific verification. Thus, "secular thinking" was a natural outgrowth of scientific modernism, the decision to trust the five senses over the spiritual sources of truth. Rather than submitting to the authority of churches or sacred texts like the Bible, modernism was confident that individuals, applying scientific reason, could find all the truths they needed to guide them through life. Science, not the Bible or church authority, was the primary source of truth.

Modernism was also confident in its ability to produce ongoing progress. Science would provide the knowledge, and technology would provide the power to assert human control over the environment. Through education and diligent effort, the human race would become more and more knowledgeable, more and more powerful, and more and more prosperous. Human beings would live longer, travel faster, work more productively, and produce food more efficiently. Life would be better for everyone. The human race needed no God to create such a paradise and no religion to provide guidance for life. Thus, modernism and secularism are closely entwined. This secular/modern philosophy dominated the Western world through the middle of the twentieth century.

Scientific modernism did not, however, prove faith to be inadequate as a means of knowing truth; it simply eliminated faith by default. Faith, by definition, assumes that there are realities in this universe outside the reach of human perception, that the five senses alone are not adequate. By limiting the field of inquiry to the five senses, secular modernism automatically eliminated faith as a source of reliable evidence for the truth. It's no wonder that secular modernism has been a significant challenge to Christian faith. When you exclude the spiritual realm from the base of evidence, you end up with a truncated view of truth.

But in spite of these methodological flaws, which seem so obvious to us today, secular modernism maintained a high degree of confidence in its ability to know what is true. Through science, the clouds of ignorance would gradually be swept away. Education would spread this new "gospel" of scientific knowledge. The result would eventually be a paradise of affluence and security. Such was the confident world of the secular modernist toward the close of the nineteenth century. Science and technology were successful enough at improving human life that they became the touchstones of the search for every aspect of truth. The tangible results of science gave Westerners confidence that they could master their own destiny without reference to God.

More recently, however, science, history, and philosophy have gotten in the way of this vision of confident progress. The butchery of World War I (1914–1918), the brutalities of Stalinist Russia, the horrors of the

Holocaust, the nuclear threat, and the rise of terrorism have all shaken people's confidence in the progress of humanity. Events like September 11 cast doubt on humanity's ability to cope with evil, no matter how much we might apply science or technology toward solutions.

Even before events began to demonstrate to inadequacies of scientific modernism, the philosopher Friedrich Nietzsche (1845–1900), the "prophet" or "grandfather" of postmodernism, challenged the confidence of nineteenth-century modernism. He believed that the "systems" of modern thought lacked integrity, since they were always based on "self-evident" assumptions. He predicted that Europe was headed for vicious wars as soon as secular modernism succeeded in ridding Europe of its adherence to the values of Christian faith. Progress and security would give way to brutality and uncertainty. While Nietzsche's post-Christian philosophy of meaning is repugnant to Christian thinkers, the power of his "prophecies" lends continuing credibility to his critique of modernism.

In due time science itself began to discover things that raised questions about its own confidence in the predictability of the universe and the certainty of its findings. Both the theory of relativity and the uncertainty principle of quantum mechanics have painted a very different picture of the universe than did the Newtonian foundation upon which scientific modernism had been based. Secular modernism increasingly seemed to rest on a naive understanding of the universe.

In particular, quantum physics shattered the modernistic assumption that human beings could fully understand the universe. There is much about the subatomic world that is not only hard to describe; it is hard even to imagine. I once played golf with a quantum physicist. I asked him to give me the two-minute version of what quantum physics is all about. He said something like this: "In quantum physics two objects can occupy the same space at the same time. Or one object can be in two different places at the same time. And not only do subatomic particles react to being observed, if I observe a particle in Nebraska, it affects the nature and activity of other particles hundreds and thousands of miles away." I hope I got that right. The bottom line is that the subatomic world acts as if Newton never existed! The lesson of "inner space" is that it offers more puzzles than solutions and more disorder than order.

And when we turn to the realities of outer space, we come face to face with Einstein's theory of relativity. Einstein disproved the scientific assumption that distance and time could be measured by absolute standards. Although many of Newton's laws are still useful, we now are beginning to realize that the universe seems to be a combination of law and chance—order with chaos. Outer space is as resistant to scientific assumptions as inner space is. Instead of an objective world that we can observe and measure, things seem to change in the course of observing them!

These changes in the understanding of physics led ultimately to Thomas Kuhn's concept of paradigm shift. In *The Structure of Scientific Revolutions* Kuhn noted how scientists periodically restructure their view of the world to take into account new ideas and innovations. The idea of steady, objective progress has been replaced by the sense that even scientists see what they want to see. Results are driven as much by the assumptions people bring to their research as by the evidence they observe and experiment with. The modernistic idea of inevitable progress has been shattered. Rather than a clear-cut vision of black and white, science today is filled with gray areas that resist neat categorization. It no longer seems a reliable source for a big picture view of reality. A younger generation sees science as just one of many possible avenues toward truth.

The twentieth century also shattered the dream of a technological paradise. Technology has brought immeasurable benefits, but it has also proven to cause as much harm as good. Scientific progress has gone hand in hand with an increase in pollution and crime. The environment has become polluted; we are drowning in our own waste. From ozone holes to global warming, the negative effects of technology have been drummed into the consciousness of the new generation. The Internet is one of the greatest advances in the history of the world, but it is also the basis for a large increase in work-related stress and new forms of addictions.

World War I, World War II, the Holocaust and other genocides, weapons of mass destruction, and terrorism have combined to wring the confidence out of scientific modernists. Technology has produced engines of destruction powerful enough to threaten the survival of the human race and the planet. During the nineteenth and twentieth centuries, scientific progress also gave the Western world its rationale for colonialism, the exploitation of more "primitive" peoples and their resources. The emphasis on individual self-interest meant that other people could be exploited as objects and manipulated for one's own comfort and convenience.

History and experience also discourage the idea that scientific progress will necessarily lead to a better world. It has become obvious that a rising standard of living does not necessarily result in personal happiness. Wealth has proven to be no shield against dysfunction, addiction, and crime. Instead, increased affluence has led to increased stress and anxiety. Instead of a new world order of peace, stability, and security, the world today seems a far more dangerous place than ever before. What used to be ordinary decisions—deciding who to marry, where to live, and what to do for a living—are suddenly fraught with huge anxiety, and a whole generation is putting off "adulthood" as a result.

The human autonomy of secular modernism no longer seems to be a life-enhancing freedom. It looks more and more like a sad mistake, a false god that has destroyed hope and led the human race into existential angst. The outcome of modernism is a loss of meaning and purpose. "The old answers and the old stories are no longer convincing, and ultimate worldview questions that once had some form of ultimate, faith-committed answers are reopened. Such reopening is usually experienced as terrifying."*

The twentieth century, therefore, was not a happy time for those convinced that we were approaching a scientific and technological paradise. Instead, a new generation looks at the god of secular modernism and proclaims it to be a *false* god. As we enter a new century, humanity is increasingly turning away from the "truth" of science to look for truth in other directions.

### Secular postmodernism

Beginning with "Generation X" (those born from 1964–1980 in the United States), an increasingly pervasive worldview distrusts the scientific approach to truth. In postmodernism, truth is not primarily found in science, the Bible, or the church. Instead, truth is found in relationships and in the telling of stories. In modernism, communities were built on having

---

* J. Richard Middleton and Brian Walsh, *Truth Is Stranger Than It Used to Be: Biblical Faith in a Postmodern Age* (Downer's Grove, Ill.: InterVarsity Press, 1995), 26.

the right ideas, ideas that the community had tested and found to be true. When people's ideas changed, they left the community. But with post-modernism, relationships and "community" become more important than the ideas that once held communities together. People can have radically different ideas and yet find community together. In the postmodern context, it becomes possible to conceive of a Super Bowl party as an evangelistic strategy.

For postmoderns the concept of truth has become elusive. Rather than "Truth" (with a capital $T$), the postmodern person prefers to think of "many truths," a "variety of truths," or "truth for me." Postmoderns feel that no one, whether scientist, clergyman, or theologian, has a clear grasp of truth. Everyone has *a part* of the picture, but that picture is made up of small bits of expertise in a vast array of ignorance. Building community, therefore, is a key component in the search for truth. As we each share the part of truth that we are best equipped to understand, everyone benefits. So, the truth process involves sharing our personal "stories" in the context of community. And as members of the community listen and learn from each other, the overall perception of truth is improved in an open discussion, and everyone benefits.

At first this postmodern concept of "truth" seems to have much to recommend it. Only an egotist would claim to have a handle on all truth. The Bible itself clearly teaches that we should be humble in terms of our own perceptions of truth (see 1 Corinthians 13:9, 12). Human beings have long recognized that "in the multitude of counselors there is safety" (Proverbs 11:14; 24:6) and that we all have a lot to learn. But there is something more than this going on in postmodern thought.

Although postmodernism is generally accepting and inclusive, it is quite *exclusive* in three areas. First, it rejects "meta-narrative," big-picture stories (like the "great controversy theme") that try to explain everything in the universe. Postmoderns believe that such big-picture stories try to explain too much and therefore promote an exclusivity that leads to violence. After all, faith in a meta-narrative fueled the brutal actions of the medieval papacy and drives the terrifying actions of al-Qaeda today.

Second, postmodernism rejects truth as an institution (such as "church"), particularly when that institution thinks of itself as unique or better than others ("the *true* church"). Thus, the idea of a remnant church is quite problematic in a postmodern environment. The church is widely associated with such negatives as colonialism and oppression. Postmoderns do not view the church as a source of generosity and benevolence.

Third, postmodernism tends to reject truth as "Bible." Postmoderns consider the Bible to be filled with violence, everlasting burning hell, and the subjection of women and minorities. Although most of these charges are somewhat misplaced, they can be a significant barrier to casual exploration of the Scriptures.

In most Western countries, people under the age of thirty-five or forty tend to be postmoderns. This younger generation will readily recognize the ideas I've been describing here. People sixty to sixty-five years of age and older tend to be modernists, whether they are Christian or secular. They tend to see things with a logical, scientifically precise worldview. Those between these two age groups, whether Christian or secular, are simply confused; they aren't sure what on earth is going on.

Sociologists disagree whether postmodernism is a new philosophical point of view or simply a reaction against modernism. If postmodernism is a new philosophical system, we will probably have to deal with it for a long time. On the other hand, if it is only a reaction against modernism, we are in the process of a transition to something else—but what? At the moment, it is clear that we are moving rapidly away from modernism, but it is somewhat less clear what we are moving toward.

Given the scholarly disagreement regarding postmodernism, we should, perhaps, not think of it as a full, complete philosophy but as a condition or a process in which the younger generations find themselves. These generations are reacting against the excesses of modernism. They are defining themselves more by what they are against than by what they are for. The identity of this new generation is not yet fixed in a positive sense. So, in everything that follows, I am trying to describe where we are right now, more than I am articulating a complete system of ideas that will govern the way people think for decades or even centuries to come. To illustrate this point I will use "postmodernism" (with a small *p*) instead of "Postmodernism" (with a capital *P*) in what follows.

As we have seen, for postmodernism, truth is not primarily found in science, the Bible, or the church. Truth is found in bits and pieces through relationships and the telling of stories. Postmodernism, therefore, signals the death of a single, universal, all-encompassing worldview. In the words of Alister McGrath, postmoderns is "something of a cultural sensibility without absolutes, fixed certainties or foundation, which takes delight in pluralism and divergence."*

One reason for the postmodern distrust of truth claims is the sense that everything one knows and believes is actually the product of one's own historical and cultural situation. Truth is neither timeless nor an objective standard. It is determined by authority figures who decide when, how, and what is to be learned. Instead of knowledge being the source of power, power determines knowledge. Questions of ultimate truth cannot be answered with any certainty. So, postmoderns are skeptical of anyone who claims to offer the "right way" to think or to act. Many have given up the search for truth and have become satisfied with interpretations of whatever they experience.

As noted above, community is now trusted to a greater degree than the ideas that once held communities together. In part, this is a reaction against the individualism of modernism. When people consider themselves free to live according to their own needs and desires, the inevitable result seems to be violence, exploitation of others, and destruction of the environment. But that is not all. A culture focused on the individual self produces alienation and loneliness. Evidently, it is not good for human beings to be alone (see Genesis 2:18)! Postmoderns are seeking a balance between the individual and the needs of society as a whole. They want to restore a sense of community and community values.

Related to this idea of community as a vehicle for truth is the idea of "truth as story." Whereas modernism was enamored with the idea of propositions and clear logical statements, postmoderns take a more "right-brained" approach to truth. It is in the story that truth is conveyed so that everyone can understand and benefit at their own level. Stories enable everyone, not just experts, to be learners and teachers of truth. This approach to truth is more open-ended than the objective and standardized tests of modernism. Through stories, the "truths" held by individuals in the community increasingly become the "truth" of the community.

---

* Alister E. McGrath, *Christian Theology: An Introduction,* 3rd. ed. (Oxford: Blackwell, 2001), 112.

## A time of transition

Summing up, postmodernism's fundamental insight is that the confident claims of modernism are nothing more than a historically conditioned construct, of no more value than the narrow-minded "certainties" of premodern or non-Western cultures. Just as "primitive" cultures were confident of their "rightness" because they were ignorant of the larger global picture, so modernism gained its confidence by limiting the base of evidence and the hermeneutic by which it allowed evidence to be examined.

Postmoderns are like travelers from some rural backwater who discover that their customs and beliefs were merely local conventions, which they assumed to be universal only because they were comfortable and familiar. Now that the bigger picture is in, there is the strong sense that modernism has betrayed everyone with a false view of reality. And to the degree that churches have incorporated modernistic confidence into their belief systems, they will face similar charges of betrayal. The following is a brief summary of some of the transitions society has undergone in the shift from secular modernism to secular postmodernism.

*From confidence to suspicion.* This sense of betrayal has led to a general transition from confidence to suspicion. *Science has betrayed us, so let's not trust science to solve our problems. Governments have betrayed us, so don't expect them to solve our problems. Religious institutions have betrayed us, so don't look for answers there. What we often call knowledge is nothing more than theories, human constructs.* Today, it's considered a good thing to question everything and to fully trust nothing and no one, including one's self. Postmoderns are highly suspicious of anyone with "all the answers."

*From stability to disorientation.* Postmodernism acknowledges the loss of any secure sense of order in this world. If reality or morality is merely a human construct, there is no solid ground on which to stand, no basis for meaning. If the worldview of modernism was simply a social construct, then it was not actually a view of reality but more like a dream, or perhaps a nightmare. The collective Western hunch that science and technology were "the answer" have produced environmental disaster, inequality, oppression, and terrorism. Those waking up from a nightmare tend to feel rather disoriented for a while.

*From one truth to many.* The sense that there is no single, reliable construct for reality has led to a focus on "many truths." Everyone has a handle on some truth, and no one and no group of people has all the truth. Although we are unable to grasp the big picture in its fullness, we *are* capable of grasping truth at a more limited level. Instead of being demonstrated or imposed, worldviews today need to be marketed in the context of many competing smaller truths. Tolerating a diversity of worldviews is, therefore, considered healthy in the postmodern context.

*From individualism to identity crisis.* If everything is just a "social construct," it stands to reason that even one's own perception of identity is flawed and/or self-constructed. The self-assured, unflappable "cowboy" of modernistic myth has given way to a plastic self that can take on whatever identity may suit the moment, but that leaves the individual clueless as to which identity is real. The positive side of this identity crisis is the sense that one can be whatever one chooses to be. The negative side is that "image is king" and that no one can be trusted. There is a hunger for authenticity but a pessimism about achieving it.

*From individualism to community.* Secular modernists pursued individualism to the point that it fragmented families and traditional community structures. Postmoderns are much more communal. They are more likely to stay close to the nuclear family, often living with their parents well into their twenties and even beyond. Through technological tools such as e-mail, they are more likely than moderns to stay in touch with childhood friends and more distant relatives. They value friendships and are more likely to sacrifice career and travel opportunities to spend time with friends.

In a sense, this drive for community is more of a reaction than a purposeful action. Postmoderns have felt burned by their modernistic parents, who sacrificed community and relationships on the altar of prosperity and success. On the other hand, the identity-less self of many postmoderns makes it difficult for them to enter into commitment or attain intimacy in relationships. So, community often becomes a wistful goal that is worth striving for but rarely achieved.

*From religion or no religion to spirituality.* Postmoderns are skeptical, not only of the religions and religious structures of modernism but also of the assumptions that undergirded a triumphant secularism. In a world of many truths and few certainties, a generalized spirituality is seen as superior to religion with its denominations and top-down authority structures.

This replacing of secular modernism by a renewed spirituality, therefore, is as much a threat to traditional religious structures as it is a benefit.

*From atomistic to wholistic.* Modernism analyzed everything in detail, from the properties of matter to Scripture texts, but had a great deal of difficulty seeing how things fit together. Postmodernism exhibits a tremendous hunger for wholeness, for seeing the relationship between objects, people, and groups. There is also a hunger for attempting to discover the big picture, even though there is great doubt whether anyone can really understand exactly what the big picture is. The independence and individualism of modernism is giving way to a desire for interaction, for relationship. The concept of "family" is being redefined in terms of "families of choice." Family is seen as where the meaningful relationships are, not necessarily as lines of blood connection. The younger generation is more interested in "being together" than in "being successful." The community, whether that means a neighborhood, a club, a Sabbath School class, an ethnic group, or a social class, is the place where wholeness can be experienced.

*From exclusion to inclusion.* This emphasis on community means that postmoderns are especially appreciative of "peacemakers," people who build bridges rather than walls. For example, they have great respect for any endeavor that unites people of different ethnic or religious backgrounds. They prefer to treat others with tolerance and respect rather than concentrating on how they are "wrong." They are fed up with religions that define themselves by excluding certain "others." They are fond of interfaith activities and seeing the best in others and in their viewpoints. They are accepting of gays and lesbians, even when they are personally repulsed by the idea of attraction to their own sex. In other words, postmoderns are suspicious of anyone who markets his ideas in terms of "us" against "them." Adventists need to be very careful here.

*From knowledge to experience.* Modernism prized "objectivity," the ability to know things as they are, apart from the way one perceives them. Postmodernism, on the other hand, prizes "subjectivity," presuming that there is no truly objective knowledge, that everything exists according to the way we experience it. Truth is not so much a list of propositions to be believed as it is an honest and authentic perception of reality as it has been experienced. "Truth" has become "what works for me." At the same time, experience teaches that what works for me may not work for you, so an experience-based truth will lead us to many truths, rather than to one truth.

*From truthtelling to storytelling.* The combination of holism and experience as bases for truth leads to the concept of telling the story rather than stating the truth. The story is an attempt to explain the big picture, or a part of it, from where one stands. The search for truth in a postmodern world involves hearing many stories. Each of those stories captures a piece of the whole picture. Every story is flawed yet is valued as a necessary part of the search. So, although the Adventist story, for example, was of no interest to the skeptical Bible scholars of modernism, the Adventist story is now a welcome part of a larger scholarly quest.

## Conclusion

Postmodernism's rejection of the Bible, the church, and grand narratives as a path to truth might seem to be a huge blow against Christian faith as most of us understand it. It is easy to question whether the hand of God could possibly be seen in postmodernism. It appears to many as an act of the devil rather than something that God could use.

The postmodern condition, however, need not be as frightening as it may seem to some. As a Seventh-day Adventist nurtured in the prophecies of Daniel and Revelation, I cannot fathom an environment that leaves God "without witness" (Acts 14:17, NKJV). I am convinced that God's hand is behind these changes in the world and that we are heading to the place of His choosing. In the next chapter I will share eight reasons to believe that God is in control of the current shift toward postmodernism. If we embrace these eight changes, I believe we will be riding the wave of God's continuing purpose for the human race.

# CHAPTER FIVE

# The Hand of God in Secular Postmodernism

In the previous chapter we saw that the world has undergone a series of major philosophical shifts. The most recent of these have left the church at the margins of Western society and have made it harder and harder to reach the mainstream with the gospel. The most recent shift is a move away from secular modernism toward what I call the secular postmodernism. But although aspects of this shift cause concern, I believe we can also see God's hand in these changes. In other words, a number of features of postmodernism have positive implications for genuine Christian faith.

## A sense of brokenness

Postmoderns definitely don't share the self-confidence of secular modernists. They are much more likely than their grandparents to think of themselves as broken people. They often come from broken homes or homes in which conflict and put-downs are continual. When they share home stories with their friends, they discover that things aren't any better on the other side of the fence. As a result, postmoderns have a keen sense of brokenness, a deep need for inner healing.

In my experience, this is as true in Adventism as it is outside the church. My own children have gone to a top-ranked Adventist day academy. Their circle of friends has included many children from broken or blended homes, with a high degree of tension, abuse, and dysfunction. Objective research consistently indicates that levels of abuse, adultery, and divorce in Adventist homes are not significantly different from those of society as a whole. The postmodern experience is fairly consistent across the board in Western countries.

But although brokenness can lead to despair, it can also open the way to the refreshing winds of the gospel. A person needs to know that he is sick before he can take hold of healing. He needs to know that he has a problem before he can become interested in the solution. An awareness of depravity is the prerequisite to the gospel. I would suggest that God's hand is at work in the sense of brokenness that secular postmoderns experience.

## Humility and authenticity

Living in an age in which image is king, postmodern individuals place a high premium on humility, honesty, and authenticity in interpersonal relationships. They feel it is better to be honest about one's weaknesses and handicaps than to craft an image or "play the audience." This principle is closely related to the previous one. Postmoderns not only have a strong sense of brokenness; they are willing to share that brokenness honestly with friends they consider safe.

Humility and authenticity are, of course, very central attributes of genuine Christian faith. Genuine confession is nothing less than telling the truth about yourself. In secular modernism humility was not prized. It was thought to be demeaning to human value. When modernism was at its height, people needed to be humble only if they had plenty to be humble about! Postmodernism, on the other hand, places a high value on genuineness. This suggests to me that God is bringing the culture to the place where it values one of the great testing truths of the Christian tradition (see John 3:19, 20). This is a golden opportunity for genuine Christian faith.

But while postmoderns prize true authenticity, they are usually suspicious of personal claims to authenticity. Authenticity is not a garment that one can put on or take off. It is the fruit of a lifelong commitment to authenticity. Many Christian communities are content to polish their image, thinking that outsiders will not see past the surface. But they are mistaken. Postmoderns can smell phoniness a mile away. If a Christian community claims an experience that is not real, postmoderns will quickly lose interest. So, there is an opportunity here, but it is not one that can be taken lightly.

## The search for identity and purpose

A sense of brokenness is closely related to the loss of personal identity. People feel broken when they have no clear idea of who they are or what the purpose of their existence is. This leads to an interesting paradox. Postmoderns long for a clear sense of personal identity, yet they question whether they can ever attain it for themselves. In their experience the identity claims of others often prove to be flawed or self-constructed. With few or no models of clear identity, postmoderns tend toward identity crisis. They may spend their lives trying on various "identities" to see which one will fit but end up with no clue as to which identity is really theirs.

This may help explain why movies are so popular with the current generation. Watching movies allows people to observe a variety of "identities" in action. After the movie is over (or after watching it several times), postmoderns role-play various characters and scenarios in their minds or even try them out on their friends. But since these celluloid identities are often unrealistic, this endeavor usually leaves postmoderns unsatisfied, unable to build an identity that will actually work for them.

This state of affairs leaves an opening for the kind of positive identity that can come from knowing that one has been bought with a price. The gospel provides a stable sense of worth that will never leave us or forsake us. A well-rounded Christian faith helps people know why they are here, where they have come from, and where they are going. The Scriptures, rightly understood and presented, provide the kind of identity postmoderns are looking for.

Related to this search for identity is an intense interest in a "purpose-driven life." Postmoderns need their lives to have mission and purpose; they want to feel that their lives make a difference in the world. This, too, has proven to be an opening for genuine Christian faith. Scripture strongly encourages the idea that God has a purpose for each person's life (see Jeremiah 1:5). If our identity is already woven into the fabric of our lives, we don't have to create an identity for ourselves; we simply have to discover the identity that has already been created for us.

## Need for community

As I emphasized in the previous chapter, postmoderns have a strong need for genuine community. I have been amazed to watch this generation handle relationships. In my generation, we liked to pair off—and not just for romance. Guys would enjoy spending one-on-one time with other guys, taking road trips together and exploring common interests. It was the same for girls. It seems to me that the relationships were deeper then, but they were also more isolated from the crowd. Once friends, always friends.

Young people of the postmodern generations seem much less likely to pair off. They tend to go out in groups of five (two girls and three guys, for example) or seven (five girls and two guys), always with their friends yet somewhat afraid to go deep. The circle of friends often shifts from school year to school year. Whereas previous generations found community in extended families, this generation seeks it in a random grouping of friends. It is almost as if postmoderns are searching for intimacy but afraid they might actually find it.

A major indicator of the need for community is the shopping mall. At the shopping mall postmoderns gather to celebrate a common passion for the twin addictions of shopping and eating out. "When things get tough, the tough go shopping!" Those who can afford it find identity and acceptance in consumption. But my daughters absolutely hate to shop alone (my son hates shopping, period, unless it is for computer games). Consumption by itself is not satisfying; it is the shared experience that counts.

In spite of its flaws, there is something very positive about this search for community. Community (*koinonea*) is foundational to New Testament faith, whether or not most Christian communities attain it. If Christian communities could learn to experience and express the kind of community the New Testament proclaims, they would find postmoderns quite interested in what they have to offer. In this area, as in many others, God's hand seems to be moving the mainstream a bit closer to the biblical ideal.

## Inclusiveness

In the postmodern attitude there is a refreshing inclusiveness toward everyone who is foreign, out of the ordinary, or just plain different. One day I or my wife (I don't remember which) made a joking comment about homosexuals. My oldest daughter reacted angrily, "Don't say stuff like that! Even if you don't agree with what they're doing, they're people, and they should be treated with respect!" I was very proud of her at that moment. She was determined not to let preconceived opinions get in the way of reaching out to others. And her comments seem typical of much of her generation.

The driving forces behind postmodern inclusiveness are globalization and urbanization. Modernism made it possible for huge cities to center around manufacturing or commerce. These large cities, the culture they provided, and the jobs they created became magnets drawing people together from all over the world. These global "mixing bowls" became the setting in which people of a variety of colors, races, cultures, and beliefs got to know each other.

Although there were many tensions in this development at first, most people learned that in order to live together you have to respect and listen to others. Postmodern children grew up, therefore, in a context in which diversity was the norm and inclusiveness seemed the best way to cope with it. The worldwide phenomenon of urban mixing means that the postmodern condition is also becoming a worldwide phenomenon, even in areas where modernism never seriously took root.

When I was doing my doctorate, the intellectual atmosphere of scholarly societies in religion seemed much more controlled than it is now. One could read papers and make meaningful comments only in relation to the fairly rigid agenda of a modernistic criticism of the Bible. People presented their views about the biblical world with a high degree of confidence. Any uncertainty they might have felt was cloaked in technical language and obtuse jargon. Most Adventist scholars felt like strangers in a strange land.

About twenty years ago, however, I was listening to a series of papers on the book of Revelation. One was couched in the highly technical language of esoteric literary criticism. I frankly had no idea what the author was talking about and had no intention of asking a question and making a fool of myself. So, I was startled to hear another scholar begin his response to that paper by saying, "I don't have a clue what he was talking about, but to the degree that I understood it, here's my reaction."

That was my first sense that change was afoot. Since that time, the scholarly academy has been much more open to a variety of perspectives, including Adventist perspectives. The inclusiveness of postmodernism has opened the way for Adventist theologians to share the kinds of insights that are unique to Adventists. And everyone has benefited from the interchange of ideas. I suspect God's hand can be found in this new inclusiveness.

## Spirituality

While I believe that postmodernism should be included under the general heading of secularism, there is no question that the younger generation is more spiritual than its predecessor generation. Twenty-five years ago, expressions of faith from athletes, politicians, or Hollywood actors were met with horror and sometimes ostracism. Avoiding religion and politics was considered foundational to public discourse. In many of the religious scholarly societies, prayer and faith talk were frowned upon, as they might be offensive to scholars of other faiths or of no faith.

But this pervasive avoidance of God talk is a thing of the past, at least in North America. Athletes, politicians, and actors are often very up front about their faith. In the scholarly societies related to religion, people are becoming more open about their own personal faith and practice—people I would not have expected this of. Although postmoderns have a strong suspicion of traditional religious institutions and the Bible, they are open to spiritual discussions with anyone who knows God and can teach others how to know Him. The forms of postmodern spirituality are challenging to traditional religion, but there is clearly a lot more faith in the Western world than was the case a few decades ago.

So, when presenting the gospel to postmoderns, it is imperative to begin with personal experience. If the truths that you are seeking to express have not changed your life, don't expect postmoderns to be excited about them. But if what you teach has changed your life and is based on tangible evidence, postmoderns will be less likely to reject your attempts at a reasoned gospel presentation. Whatever spiritual truth you present to a postmodern needs to be practical and authentic.

## Toleration of opposites

Another fascinating characteristic of the postmodern condition is its ability to tolerate opposites. What is truth for you might be quite different from what is truth for me. Yet both understandings of truth can be accepted as valid in the postmodern environment. This is quite different from the logical exclusiveness of modernism.

Philosophically, the Greeks saw the opposite of true to be false. If you knew something to be true and someone else said something radically different, they were simply wrong and worthy of condemnation. This was an important philosophical foundation for the self-confidence of modernism.

Scientific modernism was characterized by clear logic, in Greek Western terms. And Greek logic did not allow opposites to both be true. So, in secular modernism conflicting claims to truth could not both be right. Combined with the principle of doubt, this meant that science was as active in proving some ideas to be wrong as it was in confirming other ideas to be right.

But the Hebrew logic expressed in the Bible could often see contrasting ideas, not in terms of true or false but in terms of a tension between two poles. Thus, for example, the nature of Christ is not an either/or doctrine. Christ is both 100 percent human and 100 percent divine. Greek Western logic cannot allow for this; it sees such a statement, by definition, as logically impossible. Yet, the Bible affirms both aspects of Christ's nature as equally true.

Similarly, the New Testament teaches that we were reconciled to God in order that we might become reconciled to Him (see 2 Corinthians 5:18–20). That's quite a mouthful for Greek Western logic to get around. The Bible also teaches that we are saved entirely by faith, apart from works, and yet that no one will be saved without works. Even Christian moderns have struggled really hard with that one!

Postmodernism's rejection of the either/or categories of Greek logic has brought the world back to a more Hebrew form of logic. Because of this, postmoderns may actually find it easier to understand the Bible than did previous generations. The natural tensions of biblical thought seem more normal in the postmodern context. This, too, is a very positive thing.

## Truth as story

As we have already seen, postmoderns don't look for truth in the church, the Bible (as traditionally understood), or science. They look for truth in community and in the telling of stories. But this, too, is not all bad. The concept of truth as story provides a powerful corrective to modernism's traditional use of the Bible.

In the modern era, people treated the Bible as a mine, rather than as a story. It was a mass of material from which one could mine "proof texts" or nuggets of timeless theological truth, which could then be "assembled" into coherent systems. In practice, the Bible itself was not the truth; the truth was what we "mined" out of the Bible. In this process, unfortunately, it became all too easy to shape the "truths" of the Bible into the image of the interpreter.

Moderns often found it frustrating that people didn't find it easy to grasp the truths of the Bible. It would have been easier for moderns to do so if the Bible had been written in the form of a systematic theology or as a clear and logical listing of fundamental beliefs. Frankly, you can't open the pages of the Bible and see the twenty-eight fundamentals of Adventism clearly stated there. Instead, the Bible is a collection of stories and poems and random personal letters. The Bible offers glimpses of God but often falls short of the kind of black-and-white certainty that many Christians have required. Many passages and teachings of the Bible are less than perfectly clear. One might think God could have been a little more logical about this truth business!

I don't know exactly what God was thinking when He caused the Bible to be put together in the way it was, but I can only assume that the Bible as we have it is exactly the way He wanted it. Rather than forcing the Bible to say what I want it to say, I would rather take the Bible as it is and try to understand what it tells me about God. In His wisdom, God chose for the Bible to be largely a collection of stories rather than a coherent outline of carefully defined doctrine. If that is so, then postmodernism might be our best chance to fully explore the Bible's implications regarding God's character and purposes. I can't help seeing His hand in that.

But keep in mind that postmoderns value their own conclusions more than they value yours. So, they will have faith only in a story that has become real for them personally. With the help of the Holy Spirit, they can adopt your authentic stories of faith as their own. When people adopt the story of another, they become disciples, and they desire to become more and more like the storyteller.

## Conclusion

Because of postmodernism's challenges to traditional Christian faith, many honest believers feel that it should be rejected as a work of the great deceiver. But as we have seen in this chapter, the postmodern condition has many elements that are positive from a Christian perspective. God has not left Himself without witness in any age of earth's history. Now, as in the past, His hand is at work in the shifting philosophies of the time. We will be wise to take advantage of the special opportunities He has scattered in our path. That, of course, is the purpose of this book.

# CHAPTER SIX

# Overturning the Old Forms of Faith

Although postmodernism is more accepting and inclusive than was modernism, most Christian thinkers and writers are horrified about where the world is going. We must not let postmodernism's positive aspects blind us to some clear and present dangers. As noted in a previous chapter, postmodernism presents three primary challenges to traditional Christian faith. Let's take a closer look at these challenges and suggest some ways that Adventists can address them in their interactions with postmoderns.

## The rejection of grand narratives

For Adventists, a major challenge in working with postmoderns is our great controversy "meta-narrative." The great controversy theme is seen to be Adventism's single greatest contribution to Christian theology. It is certainly a defining element at the core of traditional Adventist identity. To the postmodern mind, however, grand narratives such as the great controversy theme are mere human constructs, fictional devices by which people impose order on history and make it subject to themselves.

Postmoderns are suspicious of people with "all the answers." They believe that any universal story about the world and its history from beginning to end claims much more than anyone can possibly know. Why? Because all the meta-narratives most postmoderns know about have lost their credibility. The very idea of a grand narrative has lost credibility. They feel that since human minds are finite by definition, they are incapable of creating a narrative that takes in the full measure of truth.

Postmoderns believe that grand narratives, in their claim to explain the whole picture, tend to result in oppression and violence toward those who don't buy the narrative. By rejecting the validity of all meta-narratives, secular postmoderns believe they are helping to eliminate violence from our planet. They prefer living with many stories to living with grand narratives that have so often proven to be abusive and self-deceived. They are unlikely to be searching for one set of beliefs that explains everything, but they are open to local narratives—the stories that articulate the way people in a local community experience the world. But if truth is based in community, then truth is relative to the community one is associated with.

In art, this view is expressed through the technique of collage, the juxtaposition of clashing images. Such collages allow observers various possibilities for interpretation. In architecture, postmodernism is expressed in structures that explore incompatibilities in style, shade, form, and texture.

In postmodern fiction and film, the time of various parts of the story is often unclear; there is a loose connection of ideas, and it is often difficult to tell what is reality and what is imaginary within the story. The mingling of fact and fiction even in documentaries blurs the line between reality and illusion. The classic postmodern work is the movie *The Matrix,* in which human experience is reduced to electrical signals in the brains of comatose individuals. In the movie it was difficult to tell what was portrayed as real experience from that which was only a computer-generated experience.

In popular music the techniques of allusion, sampling, and remixing blur the distinction between original compositions and reproductions. People going to concerts today don't just hear the music and watch the band; they view a variety of videos and special effects, blurring the distinction between live performance and recorded productions. Postmodern clothing styles exhibit great demand for labels that recall brand names or trademark products. This blurs the distinction between fashion and marketing. Labeling has little to do with the value of the clothes and much to do with the image they represent, which is created through marketing.

But although the postmodern denial of grand narratives sounds like a dangerous development, there is something surprisingly Adventist about it. The Adventist book *The Great Controversy,* for example, walks the reader through Christian history, showing how various other grand narratives have been the means of abuse and oppression. If *The Great Controversy* did not offer a grand narrative of its own, it could easily be described as a "prophetic" postmodern book, one that saw where things were going long before their time. When one considers how many meta-narratives *have* been destructive in the course of history, it is not surprising that postmoderns consider it better to have no grand narrative than a seriously flawed one. Is it possible to make the case for a truly postmodern grand narrative? And could *The Great Controversy* become that narrative?

To begin with, it is vital to acknowledge that all meta-narratives, including the Adventist understanding of the great controversy, are flawed to some degree. To take any other position will not only seem arrogant to postmoderns; it will, in fact, be untruthful. The Bible clearly teaches that "we know in part and we prophesy in part" (1 Corinthians 13:9, NKJV). It's ludicrous to assume that because we have the Bible we have full knowledge of all the workings of the universe. The Bible gives us knowledge sufficient for salvation but not knowledge sufficient to completely satisfy the curious. Our apprehension of truth will always suffer from the limitations of both the biblical revelation and our human ability to understand it. If we admit these limitations, postmoderns will usually appreciate the honesty and humility of such an approach.

In the context of a trusting relationship, Adventists can point out that, in spite of its profession, postmodernism has not succeeded in avoiding its own form of meta-narrative. The assertion, "All meta-narratives are false" is itself a meta-narrative. Such reasoning is circular. In rejecting meta-narratives postmodernism relativizes all other worldviews as local stories that have no legitimate claim to reality. In this way postmodernism sneaks in its own meta-narrative through the back door. Radical postmodernism rejects the universal truthfulness of every other belief while assuming its own supposition to be the only one that is universally true.

Wanting to avoid violence and oppression is good, but meta-narratives as such aren't the real reason for these evils. Grand narratives can be either poison or remedy, depending on how they are used. As poison, they harbor the potential for oppression and violence, but as remedy they have the potential to promote justice and healing. The issue is not whether Christian faith is rooted in a grand narrative but what sort of grand narrative the Scriptures contain.

According to the Scriptures, the real problem in this world leading to violence and oppression is not the meta-narrative; rather, it is the pride of the human heart. Overcoming violence requires a remedy much more radical than merely getting rid of all big-picture explanations of the universe. Overcoming oppression and violence requires the transformation of the human heart from self-centeredness to other-centeredness. Postmodernism has diagnosed the symptoms of the problem (oppression and violence) but doesn't offer a formula for curing the problem itself (pride and self-centeredness).

Having acknowledged the truth of the postmodern diagnosis of modern society, we can invite secular postmoderns to join us in a search for the *best* meta-narrative. Living without any meta-narrative is no improvement over the oppression and confusion of the past. Although we may never know truth in the absolute sense, absolute truth was embodied in Jesus Christ and can be tasted in the reality of a relationship with Him. Paul agrees that we have not fully attained (see Philippians 3:12), yet we can be on the path to a deeper appreciation of God's big picture. Through prayer, we can invite the revealing power of God to go where we cannot go, deep inside the mind of the secular postmodern. God can open minds and hearts to the magic of His great scriptural meta-narrative, if we approach people in teachableness and humility. "And the Lord's servant must not quarrel; instead, he must be kind to everyone, able to teach, not resentful. Those who oppose him he must gently instruct, in the hope that God will grant them repentance leading them to a knowledge of the truth, and that they will come to their senses and escape from the trap of the devil, who has taken them captive to do his will" (2 Timothy 2:24–26, NIV).

There are two kinds of power. There is power *over,* which is used to dominate others and to bend them to your will. But there is also power *for*—the power of the mentor on behalf of the disciple, the power that benefits others and enables them to grow and learn. What is special about the grand narrative of the gospel is that it is based on self-sacrificing love instead of on worldly power (see John 15:13; 18:36, 37). The grand story of the gospel is not about power over others; it does not produce violence. The King in the gospel story appeals from a cross, not from a throne. He is a conquering lion who turns out to be a slaughtered lamb. The grand narrative of the gospel is safe because it is grounded in self-sacrifice. The power of the gospel story is a power that is safe, a power that builds rather than tears down.

What postmodern people are rejecting is not so much the reality of absolute truth as the claim to absolute knowledge. The Bible agrees that we cannot claim absolute knowledge (see Jeremiah 17:9; 1 Corinthians 13:9, 12). In fact, to the degree we seek to defend absolute knowledge, we are not defending Bible truth; we are actually defending modern rationalism. To talk about absolute truth in a world filled with people who cannot grasp it fully is to speak in riddles.

The humble gospel approach to the postmodern concern about grand narratives is echoed in the pointed words of Ellen White to a preacher whose inward pride led him to a false confidence and an outward arrogance:

> The Lord wants His people to follow other methods than that of condemning wrong, even though the condemnation be just. . . . The work which Christ came to do in our world was not to erect barriers and constantly thrust upon the people the fact that they were wrong.
>
> He who expects to enlighten a deceived people must come near to them and labor for them in love. . . .
>
> In the advocacy of truth the bitterest opponents should be treated with respect and deference. . . . Therefore treat every man as honest. . . .
>
> We long to see reforms, and because we do not see that which we desire, an evil spirit is too often allowed to cast drops of gall into our cup, and thus others are embittered. By our ill-advised words their spirit is chafed, and they are stirred to rebellion.
>
> Every sermon you preach, every article you write, may be all true; but one drop of gall in it will be poison to the hearer or the reader. Because of that drop of poison, one will discard all your good and acceptable words (*Testimonies for the Church,* vol. 6, pp. 121–123).

## The rejection of "religion"

Postmoderns are intensely interested in faith and spirituality, but most are decidedly uninterested in "religion." By *religion* I mean the forms, the structures, the institutions, and the rituals through which believers in God have organized what they understand to be His work on earth. Such "organized religion" has been increasingly marginalized by the postmodern condition. Postmoderns prefer to search for religious meaning outside church-related activities and institutions. Their strong trend toward spirituality is matched, in reverse, by a strong trend away from structured religion with its rules, clergy, and doctrines.

The prevailing suspicion against authority in general generates suspicion toward spiritual authority in particular. Both modern and postmodern secularists believe that organized religions are coercive and manipulative. They feel that religious coercion is the most vexing of all assaults upon personal liberties. When secular people come to faith, therefore, they prefer to be involved in religious contexts where they are allowed considerable freedom in the way they think and choose to live. You could say that they prefer to be "involved" in the process by which they become converted and join the community.

This suspicion of organized religion is particularly directed at Christian churches in the Western world. The postmodern culture thinks of Christian churches as worthless institutions, willfully withdrawn from the mainstream culture and its challenges. They think of the church more as a profit-making institution than as a spiritual one. Christians are often seen as extremists who do not respect peoples' differences, who are intolerant of any ideas that differ from their church's traditions.

The impact of this bias on local Christian churches is what many sociologists have referred to as postdenominationalism. Many local congregations try to distance themselves from denominational ties in order to be more attractive to postmodern people. The institutional church is seen as more of a modernist institution than as a truly spiritual one. Almost by definition, denominations like the Seventh-day Adventist Church exist because of a claim to knowledge that is universally true. Therefore many postmoderns do not see such churches as a viable option in their search for truth. Right or wrong, one of the last places the postmoderns would expect to be spiritual is in a church. Synagogues, mosques, and temples, by way of contrast, may be intriguing to the inquiring postmodern mind.

This is a serious challenge to traditional Adventist faith. We might as well be honest. Few Christian churches are more tightly organized and controlled than the Seventh-day Adventist Church. In my experience, structures and procedures that we often take for granted are quite troubling to formerly secular people when they encounter them in their new-found Christian walk. We encourage people to become educated, for example, but then expect them to turn off critical thinking where the church is concerned. Fresh, creative ideas are frequently met with "We never did it that way before" or "Ellen White says . . ." whether or not she did, in fact, say it.

In addition, the way conferences have traditionally handled pastoral changes and local church preferences does not play well with individuals who are used to more collaborative and caring approaches in the workplace. People expect that their treatment at the hands of religious institutions should at least equal that of other institutions they encounter. Also, if large amounts of local funds are regularly siphoned off to a distant conference office, postmoderns expect that distant office to be accountable to them, not the other way around. The Seventh-day Adventist Church has a lot to learn about dealing with postmoderns in the church, financially and structurally.

The Adventist Church also has detailed expectations in the area of beliefs and lifestyle. Transgressions of both written and unwritten rules usually result in some local member trying to correct what is perceived as a threatening situation. No matter how open and authentic the pastor may be, postmoderns who feel judged and manipulated by their fellow believers would rather walk than fight for their beliefs. They know that there is always another community that might be more accepting. In the absence of strong doctrinal ties to any particular community, postmoderns feel free to pick and choose a church community based upon how open and accepting it is, rather than on the basis of what it teaches. In most cases, it matters little whether a young adult was born in a Seventh-day Adventist home or was converted as a youth; the atmosphere of the community is far more important to him or her than its teachings or practices.

The situation is not completely hopeless, however. I sense a rising openness among Adventist administrators to create more caring structures and interactions in relation to the local church. There are church administrators and structures that welcome creative, self-supporting ministries. Likewise, there are creative, self-supporting ministries that encourage and maintain a constructive, accountable relationship with the church. The General Conference is seeking ways to consume fewer resources so that more resources can be available at the local levels where most ministry occurs.

In any case, the postmodern discomfort with organized religion may be a disguised blessing. The Adventist Church should not fear the winds of local originality and creativity. These qualities are deeply embedded in our own history as a people. The Adventist Church began as an antiestablishment church. We broke ranks with all the other churches because they failed to follow the Bible; our roots are in the radical reformation. We do not need to be terrified that fresh mission strategies will somehow undermine the "system" in any ultimate sense. We have always believed that the organization exists to serve the mission, not the other way around. The postmodern condition is a golden opportunity to reform a structure that has unintentionally become self-centered and self-preserving—at least in the eyes of many who are not employed by the system.

Perhaps we can recapture some of the radical spirit of our Adventist pioneers without losing the positive benefits that competent organization can provide. It is time for church leaders at all levels to surrender their need to control everything that goes on in the church. We need to allow the creative thinkers and administrators in our church the freedom to develop more effective structures than those we now have. Simply tinkering with the "system" will not be enough to attract secular postmoderns. We need to recapture our "prophetic edge," by calling the world to radical discipleship and allowing for some "godly disturbance" along the way.

No amount of organizational change at the upper levels of the church will help at the local level, however, if the members are not genuinely open to change. If a local church is comfortable only with the ways they have done things in the past, secular postmoderns will not stay long. If you are part of such a church, serious outreach to secular people will likely fail in the long run.

I want to encourage outreach to secular people with every fiber of my being. I have come to realize (through hard experience), however, that the quality of life in the local church community will have a greater influence on my success or failure than the strategies I use or the faithfulness I exhibit. If the quality of life in your local church community will work against you, it would be better to wait for a more advantageous time or to create a new church community where secular people will feel welcome. A church that wants to reach postmoderns must be prepared to shield them from some of the judgmental behaviors that come so easily to Adventist members. Pray for God's wisdom as you address this major challenge to secular outreach.

## Suspicion of the Bible

Today's generation has many mistaken ideas about what the Bible teaches. They assume that all the ideas held and practiced by the Christians they know (or think they know from watching the news) are based on the Bible, the sacred text at the foundation of Christian faith. In other words, they assume that the ideas of the Bible rise no higher than the beliefs and practices of those who claim to follow it.

As a result, secular people tend to think that the Bible teaches many unpalatable ideas. They assume, for example, that the Bible teaches an everlasting burning hell. *What kind of God is it,* they argue, *that hides Himself in obscure texts, then demands that everyone understand and follow Him or else suffer eternal punishment in burning fire?* The very concept sounds ludicrous to the average secular person. Worse yet, it fills them with anger toward God and toward well-meaning Christians who don't grasp the negative impact such an idea has in the wider world.

Many secular people also assume that the Bible teaches child abuse and the subjugation of women and minorities. We may smile at such misconceptions, but secular people are well aware of how the Afrikaner church justified apartheid on the basis of Scripture and how many churches today seemingly denigrate the role of women in society on the basis of Scripture. They are also aware that slavery was often justified on the basis of Scripture. And they assume that the despicable abuses of some Catholic priests are somehow condoned in the Scriptures. In other words, secular people have a hard time separating the actions of Christians from the teachings of the Bible.

Secular people also take note of how arbitrary and violent the church has been throughout Christian history. They are intensely sensitive to the arbitrary cruelties of the Inquisition, the Crusades, and the Salem witch trials. These aberrations of history are featured in documentaries and Hollywood dramas. The excesses of the papacy and its administration by absolute fiat are also known to many.

The natural Adventist reaction to such charges is often outrage. *How dare these ignorant outsiders blaspheme the Word of God!* But such a reaction is misplaced. Postmoderns are not perverse in their misperceptions; they are simply assuming that Christian beliefs and practices are grounded in the Bible. In the same way, Christians make a similar mistake in their judgments regarding Islam. Most Christians assume that the radical and violent ideas of Muslim extremists are central to the teachings of the Qur'on (Koran). But such a perspective is as mistaken as are postmodern beliefs about the Bible. The Qur'on is no more violent than the book of Judges or the book of Revelation. Human beings naturally judge harshly that which they do not know or understand. So, postmoderns are no more prejudicial in religious matters than are many Christians.

At first glance, in fact, the Bible does seem guilty of many of these post-modern charges. There is the violence of the Exodus and the conquest of Canaan. There is the brutality of Judges and the books of Samuel. There are the cruelties and the slaughters of the monarchy in Israel and Judah. And throughout Scripture, women are often on the receiving end of the violence (see Judges 17–21; 1 Timothy 2:11–15; Revelation 17:16).

Worst of all, in some postmodern minds, is the seeming delight that some Christians take in the violence with which Babylon is destroyed in the book of Revelation. The violence in Revelation can't be justified on the grounds that it was written before the time of Jesus, the Prince of Peace. In fact, in Revelation, the Lamb Himself presides over much of that violence and approves of it (see Revelation 14:10, 11; 19:11–21).

Adventists, however, are in a position to sympathize with postmoderns on these issues. Our whole history is centered around the discovery that the conventional religious wisdom didn't fit with what we found in the Bible. Adventism at its best walked away from other churches when their theology and their practice didn't live up to the light we found in the Bible. So, Adventists operate from a position of strength when they draw a distinction between the teachings of the Bible and the beliefs and practices of the mainstream churches.

In order to gain a hearing from postmoderns, however, we must be prepared to hear the Bible being accused of many things without becoming defensive. Our tendency is to defend the Bible at all costs. When someone brings up the questions they have about the Bible, we tend to jump immediately to the defense. Apologetics can be helpful at some point, but it is wasted on those whose reading and experience teaches them that Christians have pat answers for everything but that their answers don't truly satisfy. Even worse, many secular people have personal stories of how particular Christians have hurt them in the name of the Bible.

Those who have been touched with the spirit of Jesus will understand that hypocrisy on the part of Christians constitutes the biggest barrier to postmoderns exploring and understanding the Bible. A change of attitude—rather than better arguments—is the key to turning this situation around. If Christians would listen and sympathize with secular people, instead of jumping quickly into defensive mode, they might in time gain a hearing for a different view of the Bible. Traditional Christianity, indeed, has much to answer for. And there is also much that Adventism has to answer for in its treatment of others. It takes time for abused secular people to come to the place that they are willing to listen to a Christian and consider the possibility that the Bible may offer a healthier approach to life than what they have seen in the Bible's followers.

I recently had my first opportunity to spend significant time with a relative in Germany. She was delightful and fun, but she had a very negative attitude toward anything Christian. At first, she wondered how I could work for a church. But I chose not to be defensive and agreed with her negative comments whenever there was some truth in them. Over several hours she became more and more open to the Bible and spiritual talk. She began asking genuine questions instead of making dismissive comments. I decided to give her a copy of my book *The Day That Changed the World,* which presents the gospel in terms that secular people can understand and appreciate. Overnight she read it all the way through, and her enthusiasm knew no bounds. I believe her reaction to an open and respectful approach would be mirrored by many postmoderns.

When secular people find out that the Bible isn't anything like they have been told, they become open to learning about it. But they are not likely to respond well to our traditional proof-text method, which strikes secular people as arbitrary and self-serving. They know that people can manipulate texts to prove anything they want. So, instead of using traditional proof texting, let postmoderns discover the teachings of the Bible in the way the original writers intended, through a more inductive, narrative-based approach. And be prepared for fresh, challenging questions triggered by the text itself. Having been burned by what others have seen in the Bible, postmoderns are reluctant to buy into a new view about the Bible without careful safeguards in how it is read.

Although Adventists are accustomed to a more systematic approach to studying the Bible with interested persons, I would suggest a more exegetical approach with secular people, particularly postmoderns. (For a detailed explanation of the differences between exegesis and systematic theology, see my book *The Deep Things of God.*) We should spend the majority of our time with them looking at the clear texts of the Bible in context, rather than debating the fine points of passages that are less clear. The clear teachings of the gospel change lives by the power of the Spirit. Sharing the clear texts avoids much debate over the Bible's difficulties.

When secular people digress to their negative stories or experiences, affirm the truth in what they are saying and direct them back to the text after an appropriate interval. Debate simply encourages people to hold the truths of the Bible at an intellectual distance. A dismissive attitude will simply confirm their impressions about the abusiveness of Christianity. Much patience and grace will be needed.

Studying the Bible with secular people will certainly prove to be a two-way street. An arrogant approach of "I am the teacher and you are the student (shut up and listen)" will not succeed with secular people. They believe in the process of discussion. Anyone studying the Bible with secular people will be confronted with fresh ideas and fresh questions. There is much to be learned in this approach. As I noted earlier in this chapter, Paul argues that people who are locked in a mode of opposition to truth are best freed with gentleness and humility, not with debates and heavy-handed instruction (see 2 Timothy 2:24, 26). The Spirit is most effective when the Christian teacher is gentle, teachable, and not quarrelsome.

We have seen that Ellen White also advocates such an approach: "The Lord wants His people to follow other methods than that of condemning wrong, even though the condemnation be just. . . . The work which Christ came to do in our world was not to erect barriers and constantly thrust upon the people the fact that they were wrong.

"He who expects to enlighten a deceived people must come near to them and labor for them in love. . . .

"In the advocacy of the truth the bitterest opponents should be treated with respect and deference" (*Testimonies for the Church,* vol. 6, pp. 121, 122).

## Conclusion

The postmodern condition certainly places many pitfalls in the way of the church. But this moment of danger is also a moment of opportunity. One could say that the emerging postmodern condition offers "dangerous opportunities" for the mission of the church. But the most dangerous position of all would be one that denies that the postmodern condition exists or that it offers opportunities for mission.

The challenges of secular postmodernism are serious. But they are not insurmountable. With more positive structures at the various levels of the church and a more inductive approach to Bible study, there is great hope that secular postmoderns will find the Adventist message relevant and refreshing. The path will prove frustrating at times, and we will need much patience, but the teacher will learn much, and the relationships that result will be deep and nurturing. The rewards outweigh the frustrations.

But the challenges may reach deeper than we expect.

# CHAPTER SEVEN

# Are We Part of the Problem?

Before we begin to talk about solutions to the problem of secularism, both modern and postmodern, it may be helpful to look specifically at the process by which an Adventist can become secular. As is the case with both gaining weight and growing up, secularization does not happen overnight, it is usually a lengthy process. It is rare that a fully devoted Adventist simply gets up one morning and completely walks away from the church without warning of any kind. Most Adventists *drift* out of the church gradually over a period of time. They may continue to believe the basic teachings of the church but progressively become less and less involved in openly religious activities on a day-to-day basis.

## From Christian to secular modernist

When I wrote the book *Present Truth in the Real World,* I articulated a process through which Adventists moved from full devotion to Christ and the church to a thoroughly secular approach to life. I called that process "secular drift." While there are and were positive elements in secular modernism (God is never completely "without witness"), on the whole this process was a negative for faith. The move from modernism to postmodernism is a more ambiguous one, as we have seen, so I will need to address that in a moment. But first let me briefly review how the original shift plays out in the life of a typical Adventist. I use the present tense because many Adventists, particularly in the southern and eastern hemispheres, are still thoroughly entrenched in the perspective of Christian modernism that characterized the church at its beginnings.

The first step in the process of "secular drift" occurs in the private prayer life. By its very secrecy, private prayer is the ultimate personal barometer of spiritual commitment. And when secular scientific thinking enters in, prayer is usually the first thing to go. Even pastors are not immune. I have had pastors' wives tell me, "My husband hasn't prayed in twenty years except in public." While such cases may be extreme, few Adventists fail to admit to at least some struggles in this area.

The next area affected is usually the study life, although for some, especially pastors, Bible study can continue for a long time in the absence of prayer. But without meaningful prayer, such Bible study will have less and less personal significance. It becomes simply something one does as a ritual or because it is part of a job description. Meaningful personal study and prayer can become absent from a person's life for years and no one else will know, except maybe a spouse. The pastor may well be the last person to know that an elder's personal walk with God is a thing of the past.

The third step in secular drift occurs when personal standards of behavior begin to erode. This is often the first clue that anyone other than one's spouse will notice. As a pastor, I came to recognize that a shift in personal standards was a spiritual distress signal. I am not concerned here with whether that person's standards were healthy or not. But when a person has believed for a long time that a particular action is wrong and then suddenly acts in a contrary manner, it is a red flag that screams out, "I'm in spiritual trouble!" The kinds of things I have in mind are in areas such as jewelry, tithe, the use of alcohol, and choices in personal entertainment. As a pastor, I would follow up such signals with questions regarding the devotional life. The shift in personal standards was usually preceded by slippage in the devotional life.

The fourth step into secular drift is slippage in church attendance. Sometimes there may be a good reason to skip church. But when accompanied with other evidences of secular drift, slippage in church attendance becomes a very public indication that the earlier steps in the process have become quite advanced. Slippage in attendance is usually quite gradual. First, the individual misses once a month, then it's twice a month, and then he or she starts coming to church only every other month, and finally, going to church just seems to be more trouble than it is worth. After a while the person doesn't even miss it.

The fifth step in becoming secular is to begin to doubt the Bible, the reality of the afterlife, and even the existence of God. The person picks up a Bible, and it is as if a voice in his head is saying, *Why are you reading this? It's just ink on a page. This is a book like any other book.* That "voice" is the effect of secular drift. It is the result of the natural influence of a modernistic, secular society that leads us away from God and a believing relationship with His Word.

The sixth and final step in the process of secular drift is an increasing distrust of institutions, particularly religious institutions. The individual becomes increasingly unwilling to allow the authority of a group to influence his or her spiritual decisions. The most interesting thing about this aspect of secularization is that it is often seen most strongly in groups characterized as "right wing"—groups that would be quick to deny that secularism could have any impact on them. In spite of such denials, conservative groups tend to manifest some of the same consequences of secularization as their more "left-wing" counterparts. In their increasing distrust of Adventist institutions, the right-wing Adventist groups and members betray that they are far from immune to the influence of secularization.

Secular drift doesn't always take place in the exact order described above. In special circumstances the order may be altered or even reversed. For example, if a person is embittered by some real or perceived action on the part of a church institution, attendance and loyalty may be affected immediately while prayer, study, and standards may continue for a while. On the other hand, a young person newly exposed to a secular university may abandon the entire spiritual life in such a brief time that the different levels of secular drift can hardly be discerned. What I have shared here is the most typical order in which the process occurs, usually over a fairly lengthy period of time.

Have Adventists been more susceptible to secular modernism than the average Christian? Many thinking Adventists, including at least one former General Conference president, have come to think so. The more you become acquainted with Bible-believing Christians of other faiths, the more you suspect that Adventists in the Western world may be more secularized than the average Christian. If so, secularism has wounded us more than once; it has not only made it more difficult for us to communicate with those outside, it has sapped our own faith, as well.

In the middle of the nineteenth century, Adventists in the Western world saw themselves as a reform movement within the larger Christian church. Most of the people they worked with did not need an emphasis on Christian spirituality. So, the emphasis of our pioneers was on assembling logical and reasonable arguments that would persuade people intellectually of particular Bible doctrines. In a world full of Christian modernists, this worked out reasonably well for a generation. But by the year 1888, this approach had resulted in an entire generation of Adventists who knew the arguments but who were losing touch with a personal God. And in spite of the power of the message that was born in Minneapolis in 1888, distinctive Adventist doctrines still tend to get more emphasis than does a living relationship with God in most parts of the church.

## Adventists and postmodernism

I find the situation with Adventists and postmodernism much more difficult to assess. First, it seems to me that people rarely "drift" from modernism to postmodernism. Although Adventists who were born at the height of secular modernism (those sixty-five and older in the Western world today) still think and act largely in modernist terms, some reflect more of a Christian modernist perspective and others more of the secular perspective outlined above.

On the other hand, Adventists who are under forty today didn't "drift" into postmodernism; essentially, they were born into it—certainly that's true in the Western world, but increasingly it is the case everywhere. These have known no other perspective. At the time of their birth, the two world wars were already history, and for many the nuclear terrors of the cold war were in full swing. Quantum physics and the theory of relativity had already undermined the assured results of modernistic science.

The "hippie movement," with its rebellion against authority of any kind and its openness to eastern religions, had already influenced the worldviews of their parents. Earth Day and the ecology movement were already decrying the excesses of modernism that had led to pollution and environmental decay. The so-called New Age movement began to affect the culture a short time later. Although personal computers, the Internet, DVD players, MP3s, cell phones, PDAs, and many other electronic inventions that are taken for granted today were still future, the decisive influences that shaped postmodernism were already in play by around 1970.

So, the under-forty generation has known no other world than the world of secular postmodernism. As a whole, the Adventist Church may be drifting into the secular postmodern condition, but it is not doing so on a member-by-member basis. The drift is more a generational shift, perhaps the greatest "generation gap" of all time. The parents of postmoderns barely know yet what to do with secular modernism, and this massive new shift is already here. And if it is a generational shift, it is not going away; it will become more and more of a factor as the older generation dies off and the newer one increases.

The generation in the middle, running roughly from ages forty to sixty-five, the "baby boom" generation in the Western world, feels caught in a vice between its elders and its youth. And this generation just happens to be the one in which most of the church's leadership today finds itself. Church leadership feels as if it is caught in a vice, and the squeeze is increasing constantly. On the one side is the pressure to stop all the changes, kick out anyone who "drifts" or is born into the wrong generation, and insist that Christian modernism is as orthodox as the New Testament gospel and cannot be altered by a jot or a tittle. The older generation (often supported by a few young adults and teens who feel like "fish out of water" in the postmodern world) is tempted to solve the problem by legislation and strict enforcement of the rules. And although that can preserve the atmosphere of a church, it would initiate a "drift" toward papal-style control with all of its consequences.

At the same time, although it may seem an attractive option to revert to Christian modernism, church leadership feels pressured by the need to understand the generational changes, to reach out to a younger generation, to meet them where they are. In the process there is increasing pressure to question everything that came to us from the world of Christian modernism—the Christian part as well as the modernism part. More and more conferences are turning over their leadership positions to those experienced in youth ministry (that's not a bad thing, only a symptom of the pressures). The church feels a strong need to change yet doesn't know how to accomplish this without undermining the core of the faith and destroying the unity of the church.

I am deeply sympathetic to top church leadership today. It is increasingly evident that neither of the approaches arising solely from the modern and post modern generations will do. Running the church today is like holding a tiger by the tail, and it is not getting any easier. It will require a tremendous amount of three things that are not always manifest in the same person or institution. First, we will need a living walk with God, both as individuals and as a corporate body. Second, we will need a strong willingness to take a fresh, exegetical look at the Scriptures and discover to what degree our understanding of the Bible has been held hostage by Western and modernist worldviews. And third, we will need a similar, rigorous openness to learn about reality, to learn about the changes in the world, to learn to discern God's hand in the wider world, so that we can apply the Word of God in ways that are appropriate to the world His hand is involved in shaping.

This book is my attempt to share the things I have learned from these three processes over the last twenty-five years of my life. I don't presume to have arrived or to fully understand any of this. But from an experience that spans all six inhabited continents and wide exposure to academic studies on these issues, I believe that the diagnoses and solutions offered here are a good starting point along the journey that we will all have to take if we want to be faithful to the God who never changes and yet presides over a universe that is in constant change.

## Conclusion

Before we get to some of the solutions, it would be well to review some basic strategies that can assist us in maintaining a living walk with God in a secular world. In today's world, an intellectual faith is no longer sufficient to guard against secular drift or the negative consequences of postmodernism. Adventists desperately need a living walk with God and a taste of His presence. There are many, many issues that will not be resolved by analysis of the world or by scriptural study alone. We need the living guidance of the Holy Spirit, as well. Doctrinal constructs by themselves may not touch the heart. As a church and as individuals, we need to go deeper at a more spiritual level if we are to have any credibility in today's world.

In the next chapters, therefore, I will try to offer some helpful insights on how to activate and personalize our walk with God in a secular world. A deep spirituality is critical to making our way in an increasingly post modern world. You cannot share what you do not have.

# CHAPTER EIGHT

# Keeping Your Balance

In the previous chapter we briefly looked at the pressures threatening to pull our church apart. In this chapter I would like to summarize what I believe is the key to uniting the church in the face of these pressures. As we saw in the previous chapter, reaching out to secular people is more complicated than just communicating with them. It is filled with danger for us, as well. Evangelistic contact is not a one-way street. We learn things and have new experiences as we interact with others. We observe behaviors that we ourselves have avoided in the past. We, too, are changed by the encounter.

The danger in reaching out to secular people is not limited to worldview and theological ideas. Reaching out to secular people encourages us to test the boundaries of our own standards and practices. It puts us in intimate situations that we might otherwise avoid. The danger here is underlined by the fact that a number of Adventist pioneers in secular ministry have suffered the breakup of their marriages in the process. Seeking to reach secular people requires an all-out effort that can leave us vulnerable to the enemy of our souls.

This means that secular ministry, whether trying to reach modern or postmodern secularists, is not for everyone. For some, it may put their very soul at risk. If you are one of those people, read this book, try to understand what's going on, and pray for those who are out there taking the risk for the sake of Christ. But if you know in your heart that you have a vulnerable soul, do not take the kinds of risks in ministry that others are taking.

Certainly, before you make the decision to engage in secular outreach, you must take this chapter and the next two very seriously.

## Two models of ministry

Because of the dangers in secular ministry, it is not surprising that the Bible describes two major models of ministry. These two models can be found in Matthew 5:13–16. Verse 14 describes the model of ministry with which Adventists are most familiar: " 'You are the light of the world. A city that is set on a hill cannot be hidden.' " A hilltop city is very visible; it is beautiful, and people are attracted to it. "That place looks exciting! Let's visit and see what's going on there." The city draws people; its presence is an attracting factor.

This metaphor of ministry is sometimes called the "fortress model." This is the typical Adventist model of outreach. Just as the lighted cities on the hillsides around the Sea of Galilee functioned as beacons for those fishing at night, the Adventist Church has functioned as a prophetic beacon to society. A fortress city has walls around it to protect those who are inside from the dangers outside. It may have its own school system and scout programs to keep the children safe. There is safety inside the fortress.

Every so often the inhabitants of such a fortress city may send out the army, snatch up a few captives, and bring them back in through the gate, slamming it tight behind them. Souls are won but not at the expense of those who remained inside the city. That is the fortress model of ministry. Evangelism occurs, but most of the members of the fortress are not required to have constant contact with "outsiders."

Although in the past the Seventh-day Adventist Church has tended to focus mainly on the fortress model, Jesus offers more than one model of ministry. The other major model opens up new dimensions of outreach to those who have felt like round pegs in the square holes of some of the more traditional approaches. Notice verse 13: " 'You are the salt of the earth.' " What kind of ministry model is this?

How does salt do its ministry? It mingles with the food and blends in with it. It becomes part of the crowd, so to speak. But what happens as a result of salt's "ministry"? The whole dish of food tastes better. The salt has an effect upon the whole. It is a quiet ministry, an infiltration ministry. It changes the world one bite at a time. Paul expresses salt ministry in the following terms:

Though I am free from everybody, I make myself everybody's slave, in order that I might win all the more.

To the Jews, I become like a Jew in order that I might win the Jews. To those who are under the law, I become like one under the law, not being myself under the law, in order that I might win those who are under the law. To those apart from the law, I become like one apart from the law, not being myself apart from the law of God but rather under the law of Christ. In order that I might gain those who are apart from the law.

To the weak I become weak in order that I might win the weak. I become all things to everybody in order that by all possible means I might save some.

I do all these things for the sake of the gospel in order that I might become a partaker in these things (1 Corinthians 9:19–23, author's paraphrase).

While the fortress model has been very successful with some people groups, the "salt model" of ministry will reach a wider variety of people than will the fortress model. It increases the influence of God's kingdom in the world. It encourages us to target specific, unique individuals and groups. But it also takes one outside the protective walls of the fortress city. And that is not only a danger to the one engaging in ministry, it can also destroy the ministry itself. Matthew 5:13 makes this point clearly when Jesus goes on to say that if salt becomes tasteless, it will become useless for its purpose. Salt that has lost its taste will no longer accomplish anything by infiltration.

Paul and James are good examples of these two models of ministry. Paul tried to be "all things to all people." James, on the other hand, stayed in Jerusalem and kept the fortress together. He boasted to Paul about the thousands of Jews in Jerusalem who were observing the law instead of doing all the radical things that Paul seemed to advocate. And James himself does not always seem to have been comfortable with what Paul was doing.* If there were tensions at times among the apostles, don't be surprised

---

* See the interesting narratives in Acts 21:17–21 and Galatians 2:1–10. Also compare the difference in emphasis between the Epistle of James and such letters as Romans and Galatians. God meets people where they are. Even in Scripture

if the biggest opposition to a secular ministry today comes from among your fellow believers.

One can find a similar contrast in ministry styles between Jesus and John the Baptist. John the Baptist lived out in the wilderness. He had nobody to preach to unless they were drawn to him. Jesus worked on a different basis. He lived, at least for a while, in Capernaum. He mingled with the people. He went from city to city. He met them where they were.

The bottom line in these two models of ministry is that we have a choice. If it is clear that God has not called us to secular ministry, we can pursue our mission in a more traditional way. God can call us to a James or John the Baptist type of ministry. That is certainly the option most familiar to Seventh-day Adventists. And it is a good option, a successful option. But if God has truly called us to reach all people everywhere, we cannot ignore the need to broaden our approach.

It would not be the first time Adventists have tried something new. When the movement began in the 1840s, Adventists started out ministering only to former Adventists. Then our pioneers broadened their approach to include people who had not heard the Millerite message. Then they felt the call to reach out to foreign-language speakers in America. And finally J. N. Andrews went over to Europe, and the gospel began truly to go out to all the world. I believe we now have entered another time when fresh approaches need to be explored.

## Radical conservatism

The ideal philosophy of life for those interested in reaching secular people for Christ is what I call, for lack of a better phrase, "radical conservatism." The radical part emphasizes being scattered out there, mingling with the people where they are. It means doing whatever it takes, a willingness to risk all to reach the lost. "Radical" means that we will make sense out there. It means to meet people where they are, spiritually, culturally, and linguistically.

---

there are differences of emphasis that some call "contradictions." But God uses the unique personalities of the Bible writers to provide a richer balance in Scripture than Paul, John, or James could have provided alone. See also Ellen G. White, *Selected Messages*, bk. 1, (Washington, D.C.: Review and Herald® Pub. Assn., 1958), 19–22.

On the other hand, the "conservative" in "radical conservatism" emphasizes being faithful to the mission to which God has called Adventists, to handle the Scriptures and the writings of Ellen White with great respect. It means maintaining a living walk with God while reaching out to those who don't know Him. "Conservative" means that there will be something solid and different for secular people to join up with.

Radical conservatism sounds like an absolute contradiction in terms. But the Bible is full of apparent contradictions in which both parts of the equation are true and necessary. For example, Christ is 100 percent human, yet He is also 100 percent divine. In terms of pure logic, that is an impossibility, yet the Bible clearly teaches both sides of the equation. We're saved by faith apart from works, yet we're not saved without works. For centuries logical people have tried without success to resolve these tensions in the Scriptures. Life is filled with tensions of this kind.

The "radical" in radical conservatism has to do with the way we reach out to secular people; the "conservative" has to do with how we maintain our faith in the course of that outreach. This chapter and the next two focus on the conservative part—how to conserve, preserve, and even build up faith and practice in a secular environment. The chapters that follow explore the radical aspect, how to effectively reach people who find your world to be totally incomprehensible.

Paul provides us with a biblical example of a radical conservative. He describes his radical side in 1 Corinthians 9:19–23, a text we have already explored briefly. "I have become all things to all men, that I might by all means save some. Now this I do for the gospel's sake" (verses 22, 23, NKJV). Anyway you look at it, this is a radical strategy. No doubt it was such statements that got Paul in a lot of trouble from time to time (see Acts 21:17–21; 2 Corinthians 1 and 2; 2 Peter 3:16). I wish Paul were here so I could ask him in terms of today's world, "Paul, what did you mean about being 'all things to all men'? How should a Seventh-day Adventist relate to such a text?"

As I was discussing this text in class one day, a student raised his hand. His name was Clifton Davis, a converted Hollywood actor. When I acknowledged his signal, he said, "I just went to visit one of my old friends in California. You have to understand that in much of Hollywood society, drugs function in much the same way that coffee does elsewhere. It sets the context for relationship; it fuels the conversation. So, my friend offered me a reefer [a marijuana cigarette]. Would Paul have advised me to take it?" (Clifton didn't actually take it.)

Following Paul's counsel to be all things to everyone will sometimes put us in delicate circumstances! Given the spiritual danger that lurks everywhere in the secular world, why would an Adventist place himself or herself in even greater danger in an attempt to reach out to others trapped in that secular way of life? Paul's answer is clear: "Now this I do for the gospel's sake" (1 Corinthians 9:23).

What is the gospel? The gospel includes the message that Jesus Christ did not remain in the isolation of His comfortable heavenly neighborhood, waiting for us to rescue ourselves. He came down, became one of us, and reached out to us in our own world, a world that was hostile to everything He stood for. By doing this He did for us what we could never have done for ourselves. When Paul acted "for the sake of the gospel," he sought to bring to the lost the great blessings that Christ had brought to him. In light of the great salvation he had already received, he was compelled to go. Thus, in 1 Corinthians 9 Paul calls on Christians to follow his example of reaching out to the lost in "radical" ways.

But Paul was well aware of the danger posed by his radical side. It is spiritually dangerous to read 1 Corinthians 9:19–23 out of context. In verses 24–27 Paul makes it crystal clear that secular ministry is as dangerous to spirituality as anything gets: "Do you not know that those who run in a race all run, but only one receives the prize? Run in such a way that you may obtain it. And everyone who competes for the prize is temperate in all things. Now they do it to obtain a perishable crown, but we for an imperishable crown" (verse 24, 25, NKJV).

Now the perishable crown Paul was talking about was the laurel wreath that was placed over the heads of the winners at the Olympics—it was the ancient version of a gold medal. "All these athletes," Paul is saying, "are knocking themselves silly for a gold medal. That is all they will get. But the Christian is striving for a medal that will never tarnish—a medal that will last for eternity." What is Paul's point? If athletes can exercise such self-control for a gold medal, what should we, who are looking for an eternal crown, be doing to make sure of our own salvation? So, alongside the radical, Paul places the conservative. You cannot separate the two, or secular ministry will not work.

Paul presses the point home in verses 26, 27: "Therefore, I run thus: not with uncertainty. Thus I fight: not as one who beats the air. But I discipline my body and bring it into subjection, lest, when I have preached to others, I myself should become disqualified" (NKJV).

Paul must have enjoyed sports, for he often used illustrations from the athletic world. In this case he mixes metaphors from running and boxing. In his outreach ministries he isn't just shadowboxing or running in circles; everything he does in training has a purpose. In his outreach to the world of his day Paul became "all things to everybody"—a very radical concept. He realized, however, that it was a *dangerous* thing to do. You will be changed by continual encounters with general society for evangelistic purposes. Paul recognized the danger and set himself a program of continual "training" to ensure the integrity of his soul. He saw his spiritual disciplines as comparable to the physical training of olympic athletes. I will offer such a program of "training" in the next two chapters.

The phrase "radical conservatism" illustrates the tension that outreach to secular society creates in the life of a true Christian. On the one hand is the critical need to get our own spiritual house in order. A settled focus in that direction often attracts the label "conservative" or "right wing." On the other hand, when we go out to do secular ministry, we will inevitably be facing difficult choices, visiting places and doing things that might make conservative Christians uncomfortable. It is hard to do that without being labeled "liberal" or "left wing." It is inevitable that the person seeking to minister to secular people within an Adventist context will be misunderstood.

We must take the conservative reaction against secular ministry seriously, however. Reaching out to people in the secular environment can place the Christian at risk. *Ministry in a secular context is hazardous to your spiritual health.* Because of this it is not for everybody. Many Adventists are better off staying "in house" for their soul's sake. Why, then, publish a book to encourage outreach to the postmodern mind? Because, then, thousands of Seventh-day Adventists have felt the call to make a difference in the secular world, which includes reaching out to family, friends, and neighbors. Because the Bible makes it clear that secular ministry needs to be done. Because the grand, worldwide mission of the church requires it.

Secular ministry can be a very frightening thing. Every day in the secular world you are faced with unpleasant choices. For example, I absolutely hate coffee. The few times in my life when I have drank some coffee, I got a headache almost instantly. So, by choice, I don't touch the stuff—anytime, anyplace. However, I also realize that coffee has become the fuel of secular relationships. The mainstream of our culture has become the "Starbucks crowd." At times my refusing a cup of coffee has created a barrier in relationship that I was never fully able to overcome. I have met people who are more skilled than I am at declining things graciously, but even they confess that knowing what to do in such situations is always a challenge. Life is simplest when we can choose between good and evil. But in the secular world we are more often faced with choices between two evils or two goods. Such times require tough and courageous decisions.

In the next two chapters I want to explore further the conservative side of reaching out to the secular mainstream. Maintaining faith in a secular world is all about boundaries. In order to reach and win secular people, we have to negotiate some of the boundaries that are natural to faith in the fortress. Full-bodied conservatives allow no breaches in the boundaries. They have a point. That is the safest course for ourselves personally. But the conservative approach also limits one's ability to "win as many as possible" (1 Corinthians 9:19, NIV). When the boundaries are too rigid, a ministry to secular people can easily become irrelevant or marginalized. There are times when we have to leave our comfort zone and take some risks if we truly want to reach people.

The problem is that once you allow yourself to negotiate some boundaries, it is easy for *all* of your boundaries to become negotiable. This is what some have called the "drive to the left." If you allow yourself flexibility in one area, it is more natural to allow it in others. This brings the secular worker into a danger zone. A great tragedy in recent years is the high number of broken marriages among those who have taken the risk to reach out to the secular mainstream. People who have been very effective in the fortress have had difficulty handling life with more open boundaries. They become attracted to coworkers, and the ministry is often ruined before it gets off the ground.

The solution I suggest is a clear focus on both the radical and the conservative in one's life. There are boundaries in our lives *that will need to be relaxed* in order for the ministry to succeed ("for the sake of the gospel," 1 Corinthians 9:23, NIV). We must be clear on what those boundaries are and why they are being relaxed. There are other boundaries, especially those regarding our own faith and family life, *that will need to be strengthened* in order for the ministry to succeed. If we pay no attention to these boundaries or if we are unclear which need to be relaxed and which need to be strengthened, we are setting ourselves up for disaster.

The chapters that follow focus particularly on maintaining strong boundaries in our spiritual life. By "strong" I mean solid rather than rigid. The rigid boundaries of the ultraconservative can become brittle when tossed into the secular world. Useful boundaries are resilient. They can take a hit and still retain their shape. Brittle boundaries may shatter under pressure. The ideal, therefore, is somewhere between rigid boundaries and no boundaries. We need boundaries that are intentional, consistent, firm, and flexible—not rigid, brittle, and inconsistent.

In some ways the chapters that follow are the most important in the whole book. We cannot give what we do not have. In reaching out to secular people, if we become secular ourselves, we will have no place to bring them. In the chapter that follows, I will focus on the devotional side of our spiritual training. It is a summary of the tools that keep faith strong in the midst of the secular world. In the chapter that follows the next, my best friend, Ed Dickerson, helps me to clarify for you the issue of boundaries—when they can be negotiable and when they must be held firm. Radical conservatism is challenging, but real. There is no other way to succeed in this kind of ministry. We must not reach out unprepared.

# CHAPTER NINE

# Prayer, Study, and the Practice of Faith

If we want to lead secular, postmodern people into a deeper relationship with God, we must have such a relationship ourselves. But this is easier to say than to do. We are living in a time of increasing spiritual uncertainty. The turn of the new millennium has produced convulsive change in every aspect of life. The speed and complexity of life are accelerating rapidly. Nothing seems stable anymore. E-mails, text messages, cell phones, and pagers mean that work is increasingly a 24/7 operation for those who are technically proficient. It also means that jobs are increasingly vulnerable to competition from anywhere on earth. Increased busyness and incompatible schedules have robbed families of stability and permanence. Where you live seems subject to chance more than intention. Both nuclear and extended families have been ripped apart.

At the same time that the foundations of everyday life seem to be collapsing, churches and other religious institutions are losing their audiences. Some have drifted into secular patterns in their attempt to be relevant. Others have reacted against change by isolating themselves in thought and behavior patterns that the postmodern views as inauthentic and irrelevant. At a time of desperate need for spiritual life, many perceive the institutions of religion as the last place anyone would look for help. It is imperative, therefore, that those who seek to reach the secular and the postmodernist be living examples of the spiritual life that mainstream people are looking for.

What can we do to counteract the devastating spiritual effects of secular drift? How can we maintain faith in a secular, postmodern world? The solution is not to take up a defensive posture, living in fear and suspicion of everyone who is different. Instead, we need to aggressively seize the reality of God's true presence in the midst of this new world. That means developing a living relationship with Him in the very places where His presence is either denied or perverted. But how can we have a living relationship with Someone we cannot see, hear, or touch? How can God become real to us today?

The place to start is in the devotional life. As I suggested earlier, an emerging weakness in the personal, devotional life constitutes the first two steps on the road of secular drift. Therefore, we need to slow down, reflect, and become attentive to His presence. The clearest message about God that most secular people will ever see is the one they read in the life of some Christian they know.

Successful relationships are built on two-way communication—listening and talking. We learn about the other person through listening, and we share our inner selves through talking about the things that matter to us. The concept of talking to God is not strange. We're all familiar with the concept of prayer. But a one-way relationship gets old and stale in a hurry. When we are dealing with a Person we can't see, hear, or touch, the listening part can be a bit challenging. So, one of the keys to a living relationship with God in a secular, postmodern world is learning how to listen to a Voice that most people never hear. The most common way believers try to accomplish this listening is through reading the Bible and other books and articles that talk about God.

## The study life

So, the place we can most reliably hear God's voice today is in His written Word and in other writings of high spiritual value, such as those of Ellen White. But not everything in the Bible brings devotional benefit. The *selections we make* for study, therefore, may be as important as the *amount of time* we invest in that study. The following will help you avoid some of the mistakes I have made in seeking a closer walk with God.

*1. What we study must be relevant to everyday life.* If your current need is recovery from alcohol abuse or from a painful past, "twelve-step literature" may be the best devotional reading for you right now. On the other hand, if your deepest need is for a better understanding of the Bible, then devotional commentaries may be just the ticket. Your devotional life should address the basic issues that you are wrestling with right now. Otherwise, it is not likely to affect your life.

*2. Devotional study needs to focus on the person of Jesus.* Jesus is the One through whom God has most clearly interacted with the human race. A focus on the person of Jesus, therefore, is crucial for human beings who want to know God. In your choice of reading materials, highlight those that help you to understand Jesus better. In the Bible, the four Gospels and many of Paul's letters have a preferred place in devotional study. In the writings of Ellen White, such books as *The Desire of Ages* and *Steps to Christ* were specifically designed to help us become better acquainted with Jesus.

*3. Devotional reading cannot be rushed.* Devotional reading should be recreational. Try to arrange matters in such a way that you don't have to set an alarm or limit the time you spend. Rushed devotionals can do more harm than good. It would be better to spend a whole hour on one text and thoroughly explore it than to read page after page with minimal impact on your life. In our technological age, we desperately need to learn how to slow down, to reflect, and to take stock of our lives. If we don't, we may find ourselves further and further from a personal relationship with God even in the midst of direct service for Him.

*4. Develop a devotional journal.* One of the most important insights of my life has come from the adage, "Paper remembers; people forget." When I read devotionally, I find that some of my most important spiritual insights flash by and then fade into forgetfulness. But "expression deepens impression." I say things in my mind as I prepare to write. I see the words I am writing. I feel the pen and the pressure on the paper. I'm bringing a variety of learning modes into play. All this helps what I write to become a more permanent part of who I am as a person.

I believe that one of the best ways to develop a closer walk with God is to journal, to write down the insights you gain from reading the Bible or other spiritual books. The best devotional book you will ever read is the one you write for yourself. No two human beings are alike. A power-packed collection of insights that have moved you in the past will be a powerful resource to maintain and restore your relationship with God in the future. You can use paper and pen or you can use a computer. In this way you can collect important spiritual insights in your very own book of devotional reflections that will make God more real to you and help you listen to His Word.

5. *Develop a reflective diary.* Another type of journal also helps me listen to God. It is something like a reflective diary. I call it my "book of experience." Most of the spiritual giants throughout history seem to have kept spiritual diaries. Ellen G. White did, and so did Luther, Wesley, and many others. In these diaries they revealed their inner struggles. They unveiled a sense that God communicated with them directly in one way or another. They charted their progress through life's challenges.

I like to get a blank journal page in front of me and ask the Lord such questions as, "How do You feel about the way I treated my son yesterday? My wife? How can I find a way to reconcile two particular colleagues who are estranged?" Then I begin to write and let the writing take me wherever it will. Often I find myself in places I hadn't planned to go but to which God was clearly leading me. At times God has impressed me with the need to express more caring to my students. At other times He has let me know that I expect too much from my children or that I have been ignoring someone who really needs me. Keeping a reflective diary, or a book of experience, can play an extremely important role in your relationship with Jesus.

## A life of prayer

When it comes to a relationship with God, talking to Him in prayer makes more sense than listening to Someone you can't hear does. Nevertheless, a personal prayer life is probably the greatest challenge most Christians face. I have felt like a failure in prayer many times. But over the years I have learned a number of things that have helped. I trust that some of these suggestions will be helpful to you.

1. *Use whatever prayer position works best for you.* There is no single right position to use when you pray. Some people will tell you that the only appropriate position for prayer is on your knees with eyes closed and hands folded. And, to be honest, that's the way I do it more often than not. But the prayers recorded in the Bible exhibit a wide variety of bodily positions. The Bible describes people praying standing up, on their knees, and flat on their faces. Some prayed with their eyes open; some with their eyes shut. They prayed with hands folded or with hands outstretched in

the air. Connecting with God in prayer is more important than the particular posture you use. Use the position that works best for you. The key is being able to focus your mind on God and limit external distractions.

*2. Focusing with a journal.* Another way to focus your mind is through the writing process. But when it comes to prayer, the writing is directed to God Himself. Writing a prayer is like writing God a letter. It can be a wonderful experience. I find that when I take the time to carefully shape the wording of a prayer, it becomes much more meaningful. The whole process of writing helps to draw out of me what I really want to say to God, things that may not have occurred to me any other way.

If the concept of a "prayer book" seems a bit strange to you, just remember that the vast majority of the psalms are written prayers. If you are into computers, you might think of the prayer process along the lines of an e-mail to God rather than a handwritten letter. E-mail has taught us that it's possible to build relationships with others even though we may not be physically together. And, for some reason, people tend to be more honest in e-mails than in any other type of communication. They are willing to say things in an e-mail that they would never put in a formal letter or say to someone's face. So writing e-mails to God can be an effective way to enhance your prayer life.

*3. Let prayer go to the core.* It's easy when we pray to pay a hurried visit to the missionaries and the colporteurs and fail to uncover the depths of your relationship with God. One reason that prayer may seem irrelevant to everyday life is because we often don't bring to God the things that really matter to us. Prayer becomes truly meaningful only when we open ourselves to God, when we share our deepest thoughts with Him. Prayer is the place where you can share things you wouldn't tell even your spouse. After all, nothing we could possibly say will shock or surprise God. He already knows before we tell Him, and He loves us just the same.

*4. Allow God to answer your prayers.* Another helpful strategy is giving God the opportunity to answer your prayers. It is easy to rush through a prayer list and then move on with your day, never expecting that God might actually respond in some way. Instead, put some paper and a pen in front of you, and when you have finished praying, take up the pen and wait. Write down whatever comes to your mind. Some of it may be silly or irrelevant. But in the quietness, God sometimes chooses to impress the heart in specific ways that prove to be divine.

I shared this idea in class one day at the Seminary. A student from Canada was moved to try it that night. After praying, he had the repeated feeling that a certain woman in Canada needed to be contacted. Since at the time his wife was in Canada, not far from where the woman lives, he decided to call his wife and ask her to contact the woman. The next day his wife called him and said that she had been unable to make contact with the woman. He urged her to keep trying. He felt strongly that the Lord had some reason this woman needed to be contacted at that time.

The wife called once more. This time the woman answered. Her response was stunning. "A week ago my husband died, and I just got home from the doctor who told me that I have cancer. I've been sitting here by the phone wondering if anybody cared." My Canadian student now has no doubt that God still communicates with His people today!

*5. An emphasis on thankfulness.* Glenn Coon, one of my all-time favorite preachers, used to emphasize Nehemiah 8:10, " 'the joy of the LORD is your strength' " (NIV). He believed the secret of spiritual power is the joy that comes from a spirit of thankfulness and praise. It's impossible to remain sad for long when you are continually reciting the ways in which God has blessed and enriched your life.

Coon suggested spending a little time each morning writing down ten things you are thankful for. During the course of the day, each of these items can become the focal point of brief prayers. "Thank You, Lord, for the air." "Thank You, Lord, for the cat (or dog)." "Thank You, Lord, for the red roses." Very down-to-earth, practical stuff. While it may sound overly simplistic, I know from experience that it works. As we thank the Lord for specific things that have affected our lives, we are filled with an incredible sense of confidence and joy. Nothing can brighten our lives like a spirit of thankfulness and praise.

## Finding time

How can we find time for study and prayer in the midst of the crushing load of responsibility most of us bear? After all, few people have the time to accomplish everything they expect to accomplish in a day. That means it is ultimately up to us to decide what is truly worth our time and what is not. You can't add anything to your life without taking something else away.

The problem is that most of us prefer not to make such choices. We try to accomplish everything that is set before us, and it just doesn't work. Inevitably, we sacrifice either the family or the devotional life—or both—on the altar of indecision. So, these days, whenever someone asks me to accept a position or perform, I ask myself the question, "What activity will this replace? Is this more important or interesting than what I will have to give up in order to do this?" If we don't choose, life will choose for us. And we will be unhappy with the choice.

All this has large implications for the devotional part of our lives. Our time with God is often crowded out by lesser concerns. So, the first step in a closer walk with God is to make it a front-page priority in our lives. The great thing about willpower is that using it strengthens it. Choose to put God first. Say it out loud. Write about it to your friends. Decide what in your life needs to go if your devotional experience is to grow. Be careful about adding new assignments or responsibilities. In the devotional life, above all other things, we must echo the words of Paul, "[This] one thing I do" (Philippians 3:13, NIV).

## Faith in practice

A living relationship with God begins, of course, with time spent listening to Him in His Word and speaking to Him in prayer. But if relationship with God is limited only to the devotional life, it will not have the lasting impact we need. Without concrete, practical faith action in the life, the devotional experience can easily become confined to a closet in one's mind. This leads to a schizophrenic existence in which faith affects our lives only for a short time each day, followed by an essentially secular existence the rest of the time. If we are to make a difference in the secular world, our relationship with God needs to be exhibited where it can be seen. This practical side of our walk with God is the topic we turn to next.

## Lifestyle matters

In his book *The Human Puzzle,* David G. Myers confirms what Ellen White taught a hundred years ago: what a person believes may have relatively little impact on how he lives. Surveys of conservative Christian churches discover virtually as much adultery, physical and sexual abuse, alcohol problems, and drug use as they find in the nonchurched culture.

The difference is that the problems are just less visible in the church setting.

What you believe may not have much impact on how you live, but the reverse is quite different. How you live has a powerful impact on what you believe. This is a major theme of the chapter "Mind Cure" in *The Ministry of Healing* (pp. 241–259). The routine actions of daily life have a massive effect on what people believe and how they feel and think.

That is the genius of the Seventh-day Adventist lifestyle. It compels us to bring God into every detail of our existence. When you're making out your family budget, the first thing on your list is tithe. That reminds you that God is at the center of your financial life. When you are shopping at the clothing store, what are you thinking about? *If I were to wear this, would it enhance my Christian witness or would it distract from it? Would this clothing glorify me or point to what God is doing in my life?* When you are in the grocery store, you are reading labels. Why? Because you don't want to take into your body things that would not glorify God (see 1 Corinthians 10:31). The Seventh-day Adventist lifestyle brings God into all the activities of daily life.

The strongest safeguard against secular drift—as even a secular psychologist will tell you if you ask—is a seven-day-a-week religion. Full-bodied Adventism is a faith that affects every moment of every day of our lives. Perhaps we should be called "Seven-days Adventists," which is actually a very common designation for Adventists in the Bahamas. Adventism cannot afford to be isolated in the closet of our own experience. To be effective in a secular world, Adventism must affect the whole of our experience in this world.

This wholehearted lifestyle is not a denial of justification by faith—it simply recognizes that when Christ offers the gift, He also makes a claim. We practice God's lifestyle because we *have been* accepted by Him, not in order to earn His acceptance. Though the apostles were clear that salvation was a gift, the great rallying cry of the first-century Christian church was, "Jesus is Lord." By that these early believers meant, "He has the right to tell me what to do and how to live."

The relationship between justification and lordship is most effectively illustrated by a story Jesus told His disciples. In Matthew 18:23–35 a king forgives his servant a debt of ten thousand talents (perhaps ten billion dollars in today's inflated currency!). The story assumes that the servant would gladly respond by forgiving his fellow servant a small debt valued at a mere hundred days' wages. There is shock all around when he does not. This story is a parable of divine and human forgiveness. What God does for us becomes a model for how we should treat one another. A balanced, living faith includes both devotion and action.

So, although devotional exercises are vital to a living relationship with God, they will fail in their purpose unless our walk with God permeates our entire experience in the real world. Through the Seventh-day Adventist lifestyle we have the opportunity to experience God at the center of every detail of our lives. Through practicing our faith, our beliefs become stronger, and our whole experience is integrated into our walk with God.

## Sharing our faith is not an option

The daily practice of faith can strengthen our relationship with God, but by itself it can become a selfish exercise. It can become all about *me;* everything I do, I do to strengthen *my* relationship with God. Practicing our faith will not be complete, therefore, until we share our walk with others. In order to keep our faith strong it is necessary to share it. Expression deepens impression. Talk faith, and you will have more faith. Ellen White expresses this idea forcefully:

> It is a law of nature that our thoughts and feelings are encouraged and strengthened as we give them utterance. While words express thoughts, it is also true that thoughts follow words. If we would give more expression to our faith, rejoice more in the blessings that we know we have,—the great mercy and love of God,— we should have more faith and greater joy. No tongue can express, no finite mind can conceive, the blessing that results from appreciating the goodness and love of God (*The Ministry of Healing,* pp. 251–253).

Can you remember a time when you shared your personal testimony with a friend or even a stranger? You told of the helplessness of your human condition. You also shared the excitement and joy that came with the discovery that Christ died for you personally. Can you remember how the act of sharing your faith confirmed your own faith? I am rarely so confident and secure in my walk with God as I am when I share with others what He has done for me.

Sharing our faith in the secular world is a major challenge. We need to learn a whole new way of expressing our faith. We need to learn to do so without crossing social barriers in ways that can end a relationship. The main point, however, is that sharing our faith is important, not only because secular people need Christ but because we also need a reaffirmation of faith. Reaching out to secular people will put us in places where our own faith will be challenged. Keeping the faith in the secular world cannot be taken for granted; it will be the result of a conscious effort to know God and to practice the disciplines of the devotional life that keep us conscious of His presence in our lives.

What I have summarized briefly here is handled in much greater depth in the book *Knowing God in the Real World*. There I share in detail strategies and experiences that have kept the God experience real in my own life. But in the next chapter we will go one step further. Even the most dedicated believer has been ambushed by issues related to social and psychological boundaries. In the next chapter, with the help of Ed Dickerson, author of *Grounds for Belief,* I will explore the role of boundaries in our engagement with secular people and their impact on the personal standards that keep our faith strong.

# CHAPTER TEN

# The Role of Boundaries in Relationships

**(with Ed Dickerson)**

One of the most distressing things I (Jon Paulien) have experienced since the publication of my book *Present Truth in the Real World* is the high number of spiritual casualties among Adventists who have ventured out in secular ministry. Some have lost focus on the teachings of the Adventist Church and have moved the new churches they planted toward a more "evangelical" worldview. Others have suffered the loss of their marriages and families. Some have found the challenge so daunting they have lost faith entirely.

There is clearly sexual danger in secular outreach. Reaching out to secular people puts one into the mainstream of society, with all its freedom and licentiousness. Secular people don't hesitate to dress and behave provocatively. They use language we may not have heard for years. They often think nothing of watching shows and movies that glorify violence and promiscuity. So, reaching out to the secular environment exposes the believer to temptations that can wear down spiritual defenses and undermine belief and practice. We go out into the world as agents of change, but sometimes the greatest change is the change that happens within ourselves.

I understand from colleagues who have studied brain research that the physical area of the brain that activates in worship is immediately adjacent to the area of the brain that lights up during sexual activity. In other words, God has designed us in such a way that sexuality, at its best, mirrors our relationship with Him in worship (see Ephesians 5:31, 32). Sex may be as close as many secular people come to an experience of worship. But if this is so, pastors and others who reach out to secular people are in particular spiritual danger in the area of sexuality. And reaching out to secular people heightens that danger. So, I repeat what I have said earlier: secular ministry is not for everyone. If you find yourself struggling regularly in areas of sexuality, it would probably be unwise to go into ministry for secular people.

But the boundary challenge is not limited to the area of sexuality. The Adventist way of life involves principles regarding alcohol, tobacco, coffee, Sabbath keeping, diet, and a host of other matters. Your convictions in these areas will be challenged on a daily basis when you move out into the secular mainstream. In the secular world, relationships are often fueled by beverages such as wine and coffee. How can you reach out to secular people and maintain your spiritual and relational integrity? How can you maintain strong boundaries in lifestyle and sexuality without ending relationships with secular people prematurely? It is time we dealt honestly with these issues.

So, I approached my best friend, Ed Dickerson, a lay church planter in Iowa, and asked him to share some thoughts with you in this area. Ed has made a powerful study of psychological and emotional boundaries; his study has huge implications for the purpose of this book. Some of the following is heavy going, but it will prove well worth reading and pondering several times over. Careful attention to the principles below will help those who reach out to secular people avoid many pitfalls and heartaches.

(From this point on in this chapter, Ed is writing, so the word *I* refers to Ed.)

### "Crushing" temptation

"I like the way the Gospel of John puts it," he said. The attractive, young single mother leaned against him, peering over his shoulder as he turned the pages. Almost in his ear she said, "You have marvelous hands. They're so strong."

It's the ultimate nightmare for anyone seeking to reach modern or postmodern secular people. The simple act of attempting to minister has placed him in an apparently no-win situation. If he doesn't say anything, the young woman he's studying with may act on the signals she thinks he's sending. If he explicitly addresses what appear to be her advances, she will be embarrassed, at least, and likely indignant. She may even turn the tables and accuse *him* of improper behavior. None of the obvious options offer the prospect of continuing a healthy relationship of any kind, much less an ongoing, discipling relationship. And this scenario isn't imaginary—it happened to me. To salvage the situation, I set a boundary.

"Boundaries" are limitations on behavior that define relationships. Healthy boundaries promote healthy relationships. Broken boundaries lead to broken hearts, broken marriages, broken careers, and broken ministries. More than one church worker has experienced the devastating consequences of poor boundaries. (For the sake of convenience, I will use the term "Change Agent" from here on to refer to any Adventist, pastor or lay person, who is reaching out to the secular mainstream.)

In this chapter I want to prepare Change Agents to understand, establish, and maintain healthy boundaries. I'll be focusing on prevention—how to protect your Christian experience, your relationships, and your ministry. Experience demonstrates that anyone working with modern or postmodern secular people will find their boundaries tested in ways they haven't anticipated.

For example, how do you respond constructively when a secular dinner guest brings wine to your home, as he would elsewhere? What do you do when a friend, who has been asking questions about spirituality, desperately wants to play golf with you but can play only on Saturday? What do you do when a non-Adventist who regularly attends your church planting wants to bring pork to the fellowship dinner? How about a secular friend who stands in line for hours to buy you tickets for a hit movie that premieres on Saturday morning? And then, after realizing you attend church in the morning, exchanges those tickets for an afternoon showing? What happens when a young adult woman begins to exhibit signs that she's developing a crush on you?

Every one of these situations—and many others—have confronted Change Agents engaged in secular/postmodern ministry. Every one presents a challenge to the Agent's boundaries, and in every case, a skillful implementation of appropriate boundaries offers the best prospect for maintaining and cementing the relationship on a healthy basis. Every time healthy boundaries are established in a relationship, the relationship becomes safer.

So, what happened with the young woman I mentioned earlier, who was leaning against me and praising my "strong hands"?

"Yes, my wife always has me open jars for her," I replied. Ignoring her suggestive posture, I talked about how Mavis is a great cook, but she often has me open jars for her. Then I chattered on about our meals and our fun times together. Shannon slowly sat up, said some pleasant things, and the study moved on. Mentioning my wife in a positive light sent a clear signal to Shannon concerning my commitment to my marriage and clearly defined my relationships to both women. I could be a spiritual mentor to Shannon, but no more than that.

To this day I don't know what motivated this woman's behavior. It could have been anything from an innocent need for male companionship—she was, after all, a single mother—or it might have arisen from her need to feel desirable or perhaps something more intentional. Perhaps she didn't realize what she was doing. But clearly signaling commitment to my wife set a boundary on our relationship and spared us both from finding out what she might be prepared to do. We remained friends and continued our discipling relationship.

Another young woman in our church planting began to exhibit symptoms of developing a crush on me. Like many young women in the transition between childhood and adulthood, she had experienced some difficulties with her father. When she gave me a cuddly nickname, I said, "That's cool. Mavis and I like to think of you as our adopted daughter too." Then I encouraged her to spend time with my daughters who were about her age. Once again I set an implied boundary that defined our relationship in healthy terms. I could be like a father to her—no more.

I could have handled these situations differently, with potentially disastrous results. I could have accused the first woman with words such as, "Why are you coming on to me?" or "It's not appropriate for you to be leaning on me." To the second, I could have said, "What's your problem? I'm old enough to be your father!" Accurate or not, such responses would likely have terminated the relationships in acrimony and mutual accusation. Instead, I was able to set healthy boundaries that converted potentially disastrous situations into healthy, continuing relationships.

Let me review the dynamics of both situations briefly. In the first case, I recognized that the woman was attempting to manipulate me into an unhealthy relationship—perhaps even without her realizing it. A direct offer of a romantic relationship would no doubt have been immediately rejected. So, she protected herself emotionally by keeping her interest vague and implicit. If my response appeared positive, she might subtly test how far I was willing to go. If I responded negatively, she could deny her intentions and accuse me of reading more into her actions than she intended. For me, it was potentially a no-win situation.

But in order to be manipulated, we have to cooperate with the manipulator. So, instead of receiving the unspoken signals, I responded to her implied offer by setting an *implied boundary.* Instead of saying "I'm a married man"—an explicit boundary—I simply alluded to my married status by mentioning my wife and describing my marriage in positive terms. Without declaring "I'm happily married and not available," which would have been awkward, at best, I managed to communicate the same message by implication, sparing everybody significant discomfort. So much so that I doubt she even remembers the incident today.

In the second situation, I recognized that this young woman's difficulties with her father were behind her attempts to find a replacement for his approval and affection. Once again, I proactively defined our relationship in healthy terms, as a father/daughter relationship, further defining it by explicitly including my wife and daughters. Her cuddly nickname for me was not an implied offer but more an ambiguous expression of her need for male affection. By my implied boundary, I simply channeled her needs into an appropriate mode of expression.

Anyone can set and maintain effective boundaries once they know how—if they want to. The next few pages will provide an overview of the "know-how." But first, some definitions.

## Boundaries: eight areas

The Change Agent needs to be aware of eight boundary areas, as follows:

| Vital Boundaries | | Instrumental Boundaries | |
| --- | --- | --- | --- |
| These form the substance of life itself. Remove any one of them, and life ceases to exist. | | These are how we express the substance of our lives, specifically the boundary immediately to the left. | |
| 1. *Beliefs* What's worth dying for | Also called *convictions*. Determine which things/ideas/people are worth dying for. Often stir the emotions, but mainly rational. Should be highly durable due to repeated testing. | 5. *Feelings* | Also called *emotions*. Not rational. Transitory. Sometimes mistaken for beliefs. |
| 2. *Life* What makes life worth living | Those choices, directed by beliefs and informed by preferences, that determine your life's path. Education, vocation, marriage, location, etc. Reflect our deepest sense of uniqueness. | 6. *Preferences* | Expressions of our uniqueness. Choices that are personal and have no moral content. Favorite color, food, sport, scenery, etc. Worship expressions come in here. |
| *The above boundaries are essentially totally internal. No one can affect them except as we give consent and cooperation. Those below are increasingly available to the public. They are the avenues people use to try to manipulate our upper group of boundaries.* | | | |
| 3. *Body* | Includes appropriate touch, sexuality; our intimate possessions (wallet/purse), clothing, dwelling, vehicle. Our private spaces. Includes exercise, sleep, hygiene, etc. | 7. *Reputation* | Both what others think of us and our own self-image. |
| 4. *Time* | The key boundary. Just as the key to your home is far from the most valuable item you own, yet it still gives access to everything else, so your time is the key to all the other boundaries. | 8. *Possessions* | The tangible things that we own. Vehicles for, or obstacles to, our true purpose. |

You will notice that these eight boundaries can be grouped in two dimensions—the vertical axis distinguishing between vital and instrumental boundaries and the horizontal axis separating internal and external boundaries (I'll explain in a minute). They are also numbered in the order of their importance to one's spiritual and emotional health. Beliefs—boundary no. 1—is the most important; Life—boundary no. 2—is the second most important, etc.

Boundaries in the right-hand column of the chart above are the practical extensions of those in the left-hand column. For example, a belief (boundary no. 1) that something is wrong often first manifests itself as a feeling (boundary no. 5) of discomfort or repulsion. Life choices (boundary no. 2) are often reflected in preferences (boundary no. 6).

When they are healthy, instrumental boundaries act as an early warning system, an advanced defense perimeter. We've already mentioned that an initial feeling (boundary no. 5) of unease may signal something that, upon reflection, we realize violates or threatens our beliefs (boundary no. 1). Invoking an instrumental boundary is generally less threatening than to invoke a vital boundary; instrumental boundaries can be employed proactively with little adverse effect. For example, saying "I don't feel good about this" doesn't carry the same weight—or implied threat—as saying "I believe this is wrong." Some situations will require setting drastic boundaries, of course, but generally it's better to set the gentler boundaries and set them sooner.

Violation of our internal boundaries usually requires our explicit consent. So, people who want to manipulate us almost always begin with our external boundaries (body, time, reputation, and possessions) where they have more freedom of action and where our responses tell them how difficult it will be to manipulate us further.

Adventist standards in areas such as diet and dress involve both vital and instrumental boundaries. They are the outward expressions of our beliefs and inner life, but they are also somewhat dependent on time and place. For example, some specific details of fashion do not involve absolute right or wrong—as Ellen White's experiences with "dress reform" illustrates. Most cultures consider bare ankles for women to be modest, but others consider it scandalous. Strict Islamic cultures regard baring even a few strands of feminine hair as scandalous, while in most other cultures exposing a woman's hair is taken for granted as normal and modest.

Fundamental principles of simplicity, economy, and modesty, then, are crucial in the area of dress. These principles operate at the level of beliefs (boundary no. 1) and life (boundary no. 2). They cannot be compromised or negotiated without grave spiritual peril. However, how we express these principles in terms of practical details (feelings, boundary no. 5; preferences, boundary no. 6; and reputation, boundary no. 8) may differ at various times and in various places. When it comes to Adventist standards, therefore, Change Agents must preserve inviolate their core principles at the level of "beliefs" and "life" while being flexible concerning the expression of those principles. The following definitions will help clarify these issues for readers interested in reaching out to modern and postmodern secular people.

## Definitions

*Acceptance.* Healthy boundaries include accepting other people as they are. This is unconditional love, which I define as follows: "I love you as you are. You need not change to receive my love, and if you change, you will not forfeit my love." This is at the heart of the gospel and at the heart of every healthy relationship, as well. Attempting to change people is manipulation, the antithesis of acceptance. The flip side of acceptance is confrontation. Without this aspect, acceptance becomes mere indulgence. Our outreach to secular people must be rooted in acceptance, a passionate love for the lost—a love that is not conditioned on whether the other person responds to our outreach.

*Boundaries.* Boundaries are limitations on behavior—both our own and others—that define relationships. Natural boundaries function very much like our conscience, distinguishing between good and bad behaviors and attitudes. And like our conscience, if we allow these boundaries to be repeatedly violated, they will no longer function as the safeguards we need. Boundaries first originate and exist in our minds. We choose how we treat others and how we will allow them to treat us. *Boundaries always go both ways.* What we allow ourselves to do to others, we will eventually allow others to do to us.

*Boundary setting.* Boundary setting occurs when we notify others of the behavior limitations we have already set in our own minds. We can set boundaries in formal ways or more informally. We can make them bluntly clear or leave them implied. Boundary setting helps a healthy relationship stay on track and helps a troubled relationship to get back on the right track. Boundary setting should be as painless as possible but as clear as necessary because *boundaries always go both ways.* We need to be clear about boundaries in our own minds first. We need to know which principles are vital to our Adventist faith and which are negotiable in a particular situation. Then we can set boundaries that are as painless as possible yet as clear as necessary.

*Confrontation.* To confront someone is to discover the truth about a relationship. Confrontation does not mean "setting the other person straight." It does not mean telling them off or attempting to change their behavior. Confrontation does not even have to mean conflict. Confrontation results in conflict only when issues have piled up between us to the point that conflict is inevitable.

Boundary setting is a form of confrontation because it clarifies the truth about a relationship. My implied boundaries with the two women mentioned earlier revealed a truth about our relationships, about what they could be, and what they would not be. Relationships without confrontation are relationships without boundaries. Therefore, *there are no healthy relationships without confrontation.*

*CUP.* I use the acronym CUP to express the three qualities that encourage a high sense of self-worth in a person. A person has a high sense of value or personal worth in God's sight when he knows he is (1) capable (useful to God and others in light of the gifts he has received from the Spirit), (2) unique ("There is no one else just like me"), and (3) precious (valuable to God and others). When we know in our heads and feel in our hearts that we are capable, unique, and precious, we have a full CUP.

A full CUP is the continuing awareness of our infinite value in God's sight (precious), the honor and importance of our unique calling (unique), and a recognition of God's continuing presence in our efforts (capable). This CUP can be filled in many ways, but maintaining boundaries and including sufficient time for devotions, family, exercise, and sleep are minimums. The more our CUP is full, the stronger our natural boundaries will be.

On the other hand, people who have been abused and violated have an empty CUP and poor boundaries. Once we have been violated, it is much easier to allow others to violate us again. For a person with an empty CUP, planting a church or trying to evangelize secular people will likely result in disaster. Ironically, people with empty CUPs are often attracted to ministry as a way to fill their CUPs. But ministry will be unsatisfying and unsuccessful if the CUP is empty. "Fill my cup, Lord" comes first; only then will I have something with which to fill others. First things first.

*Explicit boundary.* An explicit boundary is a direct "in your face" declaration of the boundary. It can be done in a formal way, as in an announcement or a written policy; or in an informal way, as in an oral statement between two people. Explicit boundaries work well as policy statements. In interpersonal relationships, explicit boundaries tend to be more adversarial in nature than implied boundaries, especially in otherwise shallow relationships. In personal relationships they will often be used to remedy specific problems: "I must ask you not to call me after 9:00 P.M."

*Formal boundary.* Formal boundaries include policy booklets, mission statements, and core values. Although mission statements and core values are positive formal boundaries that focus group efforts, most formal boundaries are set as the result of failed personal relationships. In a group setting, the practice of making a rule—a formal boundary—for everyone because of the behavior of a single individual, may be a common response, but it is generally a mistake. Because it avoids direct confrontation with the individual regarding the behavior, it tends to spread the unhealthy personal relationship to the entire group.

Secular people often react negatively to formal boundaries in personal relationships, so they should be used with care and only when other types of boundaries have failed.

*Implied boundary.* Implied boundaries are set when we allude—either directly or indirectly—to what a proper relationship would be like. An implied boundary minimizes the risk of making the relationship adversarial. Everyone can retreat from the confrontation without losing face. It can be done with humor and can be expressed as an affirmative rather than a negative. People with good boundaries will intuitively respect these. People who ignore implied boundaries have poor boundaries themselves because *boundaries always go both ways.* The Change Agent should be on guard whenever he encounters someone who ignores implied boundaries, because these are deeply wounded people who are likely to deeply wound others.

*Informal boundary.* Unless it's a contract, property line, marriage license, or other legal instrument, virtually every boundary between two individuals in their personal relationships is an informal boundary. In general, boundaries in personal relationships become formalized only after some breach occurs in the relationship. For example, the formal boundary of divorce occurs only after long and repeated breakdowns in the personal relationship.

*Instrumental boundaries.* Instrumental boundaries are the practical, everyday means we use to realize and express our vital boundaries. Often these instrumental boundaries warn us of deeper potential violations. For example, we may "feel" (boundary no. 5) that something is wrong (a violation of our beliefs, boundary no. 1) before we can think it through. Even though feelings are not reliable indicators of intellectual truth, they cannot be simply ignored or violated with impunity. For a person with a full CUP and healthy boundaries, feelings are a wonderful early warning system that something is wrong in a relationship.

Similarly, our life choices of spouse and vocation (boundary no. 2) are deeper expressions of our preferences (boundary no. 6). We often feel most affirmed when someone remembers these preferences. And someone who carelessly violates our preferences will also be willing to dictate our life choices. More than one case of sexual infidelity (a violation of boundary no. 3, body) would have been avoided if those involved had been more careful about reputation (boundary no. 7).

*Manipulation.* Manipulation violates boundaries by stealth. The manipulator attempts to steal choices from the one being manipulated, without being seen to do so. The serpent manipulated Adam and Eve, making them choose him instead of God. As a consequence of sin, manipulation has become standard operating procedure for most human relationships. Manipulation has even infiltrated evangelism and discipling, with disastrous consequences. Manipulating people into baptism through fear means they bring that fear, and the habit of manipulating, into the church. We should not be surprised, then, if a more skillful manipulator, like David Koresh, one day manipulates them into leaving the church.

Ridding your life and your ministry of manipulation resembles ridding your lawn of dandelions, except that some homeowners actually do get rid of dandelions. But you must make a continual effort because habitual manipulation erodes boundaries and sooner or later will threaten the integrity of your ministry. *Like boundaries, manipulation always goes both ways. The manipulator is also being manipulated.*

There are three primary modes of manipulation (these are based on Stephen Karpman's *Drama Triangle*). The "Persecutor" uses intimidation to get his or her way. The "Rescuer" uses good intentions to manipulate. And the "Victim" uses suffering to shape how others respond to him or her. Skilled manipulators rapidly shift among all three roles as a situation unfolds. One such manipulator, called to account for dishonesty in a school-hiring situation, managed all three in a single sentence. "The school board is not answerable to you [attempted intimidation and false in this case because the school board *was* subordinate to the church board]. I was just doing my best to help the school [good intentions], I work so hard for the school that I don't deserve to be criticized ["suffering"]." All this in response to a simple question: "Did you tell the church board . . . ?"

*Remedial boundaries.* A breach in a relationship requires a remedial boundary that is explicit and often expressed in the negative—"Please don't call me late at night again." Or in terms of remedial action to be taken—"From now on, I will have to leave our studies promptly at 3:00 P.M."

Implementing a remedial boundary incurs the greatest risk that the relationship will become adversarial. Yet, once damage has occurred, remedial boundaries offer the only hope of true reconciliation. They must be implemented, but they are the most difficult and unpleasant boundaries to set. It is much better to confront the other party *before* damage occurs, emotions are aroused, and the stakes are raised.

As a consequence of the pain that accompanies boundary violations, you will be tempted to retaliate. ("I'm sick and tired of you calling me at all hours to whine!" Or, "You waste too much time getting around to what's bothering you.") Besides being wrong, retaliation thoroughly muddles the relationship and makes reconciliation maddeningly complex. However, relationships that survive both the boundary violation and the remedial boundary setting will emerge stronger than ever. When they truly heal, broken relationships heal like broken bones, knitting together stronger at the site of the break.

*Roles and relationships.* In life we constantly change roles. Each role—pastor, employee, father, husband, coworker—has its own set of boundaries. Many relational problems arise from forgetting in which role we are acting. Acting as a pastor toward one's spouse, for example, won't work at home.

*Unbalanced relationships.* Truly unbalanced relationships are unhealthy. But this term can refer to a class of relationships in which one party has more power than the other, such as parent/child, teacher/student, counselor/client, etc. To keep such relationships balanced and healthy, we offset the greater power by imposing greater responsibility on the more powerful party. Discipling relationships fall into this category, meaning that the Change Agent bears an extra burden of responsibility in outreach relationships. To mitigate the effects of this stress, the Agent must take extra care to keep his or her CUP full.

*Vital boundaries.* These four boundary areas (Beliefs, Life, Body, and Time) form the inner sanctum of your life. In a sense, they *are* your life. These must be compromised only in extreme situations. For example, one might permit a limb to be amputated or an organ to be removed in order to preserve life. Or one might be required to give up life itself to maintain a belief or a conviction.

Beliefs are the most vital boundary, and they must not be compromised. But this is an area where a lot of confusion can come in. We must carefully distinguish beliefs from feelings, preferences, or even reputation. A person who elevates a feeling or a preference to belief status could end up dying for something that is not vital to the core of his or her being. And we must not allow our beliefs to become demands on others. My belief obligates *me*. It places no obligation on others.

## Boundaries and secular outreach

*Choosing to be a Change Agent.* Choosing to be a Change Agent in the secular world springs from the individual's deepest beliefs and life choices. That is, I accept the call to spend my life sharing my beliefs with a nonbelieving community. Since beliefs represent those values worth dying for and life choices represent those things which most make life worth living, this provides powerful motivation. To be effective the Agent will have to be willing to sacrifice some of the lower priority boundaries (nos. 5–8) in order to preserve the higher priority ones.

One of the challenges that comes when an Adventist reaches out to the secular mainstream is that Adventists often equate specific standards with vital beliefs. The Change Agent must be prepared for a great amount of criticism from people not operating at the same level of analytical thinking. Change Agents will need to be as patient with fellow believers as we must be with modern and postmodern secular people.

*Beliefs, feelings, and preferences.* It's extremely important that the Agent recognize the difference between his beliefs and feelings, his life choices and his preferences. Worshiping God is a conviction, but exactly *how* we express worship is a matter of preference. Do we pray standing, with arms outstretched? Or prone on a prayer rug? Be aware that the same pipe organ music that says "majestic" to me says "funeral" to someone else. In our ministry to secular and postmodern people, we will have to forego many of our preferences. To balance this, it becomes imperative that in our private and family time, we humor those preferences. Otherwise, our CUP will begin to seem empty.

No matter how thoroughly you prepare, it will be impossible to anticipate every challenge that secular ministry will pose to your beliefs. So, it is extremely important that you possess a strong sense of identity as a Seventh-day Adventist Christian, a robust personal theology, and the ability to distinguish between beliefs, feelings, and preferences. Many a church "standard" is simply someone's strong preference masquerading as a belief.

*Resilient, not rigid.* When speaking about robust boundaries, it's important to note that this emphatically does *not* mean detailed lists of activities and sets of circumstances. Such lists tend to be digital in nature: on/off; yes/no; light/dark; living/dead; either/or. On the other hand, real life tends to be analog, a continuum of bad, poor, fair, good, better, and best. In the new earth, we will enjoy only the best. In this broken and sinful world, sometimes the Change Agent must venture down the scale, perhaps sometimes as far as "poor" in order to reach the lost.

The notion of compromise no doubt raises concerns. But even God compromises in order to meet people where they are. In the five books of Moses, God compromised on slavery (see Exodus 20:10, 17) and divorce (see Deuteronomy 24:1–4; cf. Genesis 2:24). Although both were clearly contrary to His will, He allowed them to continue but provided remedies for their worst abuses (see Exodus 21:1–6; Deuteronomy 24:1–4). Admittedly, this "sliding scale" approach generates some serious hazards.

| RIGHT | R/W? | R/W? | R/W? | R/W? | WRONG |
|-------|------|------|------|------|-------|
| Best | Better | Good | Fair | Poor | Bad |

On the other hand, digital "standards" bring problems of their own. Lists of rules don't prove effective as boundaries. Quite the contrary. In practice, such legalistic efforts are rigid and brittle. On the scale above, how far to the right can one go before reaching "wrong"? Rigidity prevents us from moving far enough down the scale from "best" to reach many people. But if we allow "poor" to be "right," in a particular case, then why is that "poor" option not always right? Such brittle either/or boundaries cannot be easily repaired. The Agent may feel he has violated his conscience, despair, and lose hold on faith. By contrast, remaining flexible and realizing why a stretch was made to accommodate an option that was not the best allows one to reach the lost and still maintain one's personal experience. I may do something for another that I would not do for myself. Jesus healed others on the Sabbath, but He did not take up His own life until the Sabbath hours had passed. Paul recognized this principle in 1 Corinthians 9:19–27.

Healthy boundaries are tough and resilient; they can take a hit and bounce back. That's important, because in a sinful world they'll take plenty of hits. The Bible refers to a hedge, especially a hedge of thorns, as a barrier against Satan (see Hosea 2:6, 7). Even today, a hedge of thorns is not a boundary to be taken lightly.

The fortifications of concrete and steel that guarded the Normandy beaches on June 6, 1944, held up the massive Allied invasion force less than twelve hours. But the French hedgerows held back the burgeoning force of men and armor for weeks. Return to that area of France today, and you will notice in the hedgerows little evidence of the shots, shells, and blood expended there. They simply grew back. Healthy boundaries can take hits and survive. Brittle, rigid boundaries are shattered and destroyed.

## A strategy for restoring boundaries

Boundary problems arise for many reasons. If a person realizes he has difficulties in the area of boundaries, how can he reestablish, restore, and strengthen them? There are four main steps that any Change Agent will want to keep in mind at all times in secular outreach:

- Keep your "CUP" filled.
- Be aware of the potential dangers in each situation.
- Be aware of the unique secular/postmodern challenges.
- Be intentional and proactive in setting boundaries.

*Keep your CUP filled.* Boundaries do not exist for their own sake. The key boundary is time. Just as the key to your house gives access to the walls, the attic, the floor, and every precious thing they shelter, the time boundary gives access to every one of your boundaries and to what they shelter.

No matter how strong the demands of ministry, always allocate adequate time to your Lord, yourself, and your family. There's a reason God reserves one-seventh of your time and only one-tenth of your money. God knows that healthy relationships demand time and lots of it. And forget the notion of quality time; time is like gold ore—you get so much gold per ton. Do you want more gold? Process more ore! Do you want better relationships? Spend more time on them.

Maintaining a balanced life is not a distraction from ministry—it is the essence of ministry. If salvation means having a saving relationship with God, ministry is the business of helping people build saving relationships. Don't forget, "everyone who is fully trained will be like his teacher" (Luke 6:40, NIV). If dedication to ministry results in seriously unbalanced relationships, then those you disciple will emulate those unbalanced relationships. As they join your ministry, this will institutionalize these relationship defects, which then become defining characteristics of the ministry. *Defective boundaries always go both ways. The one whose boundaries are violated will violate the boundaries of others.*

*Be aware of potential dangers.* The tempter always works on some genuine weakness in our system of values; he offers to satisfy some need we have starved. God intended for Eve to eat to satisfy her hunger. It wasn't feeding her hunger that was sin; it was using the illicit means of forbidden fruit to feed it. If your God-given hungers are met with appropriate food, you will be less likely to seek forbidden fruit.

With our own needs met, we will be more alert to potential dangers. Change Agents work with broken and hurting people, people whose boundaries are broken and whose CUPs are empty. Such people will quickly look to us to fill their needs.

Since we all lack perfection, we all have unmet needs. It is imperative that Change Agents be doubly alert in areas where they personally struggle. Awareness of our own weaknesses should inspire not fear, but humility; not despair, but caution. Like a good defensive driver, the Change Agent should be aware not only of hazards directly in front of him or her but of potential hazards well down the road.

*Secular/postmodern challenges.* In this broken world, we all have broken boundaries. But the boundaries of postmoderns are especially battered. This can be attributed to several causes. Contemporary society prides itself on breaking down boundaries. In particular, the younger generation in the Western world has suffered the breakdown of nearly every significant institution in their lives—broken homes, government corruption, and assault on traditional values. Generation X (those born from 1964 to 1980) is the most aborted, abused, molested, and neglected generation in recent history.

Change Agents must realize that the poor boundaries of postmodern individuals mean that they will readily violate the boundaries of the Agent. Beyond this, they will be highly sensitive and easily offended when the Agent establishes boundaries. So, great care must be exercised to protect everyone involved. Since the primary responsibility for safeguarding a mentor/disciple relationship is on the mentor, Change Agents need to master the principles involved in setting and maintaining boundaries.

*Intentional and proactive boundary setting.* Not only does the traditional witnessing approach of systematically presenting propositional truths fail to attract secular postmoderns, it actively offends them. Talk about sex all you want, using the crudest language, and few will be offended. But talk about right and wrong, about convictions and beliefs, and postmoderns will react as if you had committed a public indecency. They simply do not talk about such things seriously, even among themselves, except in the most intimate of relationships, and not without discomfort even then. There is the correct sense that abuse in the name of religion is the greatest of all abuses because it violates the most vital of all boundaries—beliefs.

Opportunities for ministry, therefore, must be earned in all outreach to secular people, particularly the younger, more postmodern type of secular person. If you want to share beliefs with postmoderns, you must first build a relationship of trust and allow them to share their beliefs, as well. Boundaries always go both ways.

Postmoderns will not readily define their relationship with you; it seems too much like a commitment, something they scrupulously avoid. So, it will be up to the Agent to do so. This must be done with the utmost subtlety and tact in order not to scare the secular postmodern individual out of the relationship altogether.

Accordingly, in the early stages of relationship (see the stages of friendship in chapter 16), be prepared to proactively define the relationship by referring to healthy models. At first, speak solely in terms of the boundaries on the right side of the chart on page 108 (boundaries nos. 5–8). Instead of saying "I keep the *true* Sabbath" (a belief statement), say "I choose to reserve Saturdays as my spiritual time" (a preference statement). In discussing doctrine, speak in terms of feelings (boundary no. 5) more often than beliefs (boundary no. 1). When speaking of beliefs, speak tentatively. Telling people what they should believe is, in fact, a boundary violation and should be avoided. But with secular postmoderns, it may well end the relationship.

## Conclusion (Jon Paulien)

Ministry to modern and postmodern secular people will confront you at every point. But this is good news. Since there are no healthy relationships without confrontation, such a ministry will be an extraordinary opportunity for personal growth. The very challenges that make the ministry difficult also make it fruitful for us spiritually. It will push us to lean more heavily on God and to trust less in ourselves. And as our own boundaries are strengthened through nurture and practice, we will experience a joy in life and faith that we never knew before.

Secular ministry is not for everyone. It will challenge every boundary. But to those who have heard God's call to be "Change Agents" in the mainstream culture, it can be a road to a deeper and more fulfilling spiritual life.

# CHAPTER ELEVEN

# Living Like Salt in a Secular Postmodern World

As we have seen, the Bible describes two major models of ministry. Matthew 5:14 uses the figure of a fortress city to illustrate a community that is visible, attractive, and yet carefully protected. The city draws people into itself; its presence is an attracting factor. It doesn't try to change the world around it; it calls people out of that world. Matthew 5:13, on the other hand, uses the figure of salt to illustrate a community that goes out and mingles with others in a desire to do them good. Just as salt performs its task by blending into a dish of food, so the church, as salt, infiltrates the world and changes it (see 1 Corinthians 9:19–23).

The fortress model of ministry is safer for those who are inside the fortress, but the salt model of ministry will reach more people. It's not a matter of either/or. Both models of ministry are useful, and both models are needed. For those who need the safety that the fortress provides, it is the preferred model of ministry, as is generally the case with Adventist outreach. But the fortress model places natural limits on the effectiveness of the outreach. Many segments of society today can be reached only through a salt approach. This is particularly true with the target audiences being discussed in this book—modern and secular postmoderns. If we want to reach the mainstream of Western society, we will need to explore what it means to be salt in the world.

The call to a salt ministry is a call to radical conservatism. It is a call to be more conservative than ever in one's personal life and integrity in order to survive the challenges that come when you go on secular turf. It is a call to follow the example of Paul who tried to be "all things to all people." It is a call to follow the example of Jesus, who mingled with prostitutes and swindlers, who traveled from city to city and met people where they were yet retained His purity of heart. It is a call to follow the examples of Enoch, Joseph, Daniel, and Esther. The way is not easy, but love for the lost will invite us to take the harder road, if necessary, in order to win as many as possible.

The bottom line in these two models of ministry is that we have a choice. If it is clear that God has not called us to secular ministry, we can pursue our mission in a more traditional way with a clear conscience. But if God has truly called us to reach all people everywhere, we cannot ignore the need to broaden our approach. We will be following the examples of people like J. N. Andrews, L. R. Conradi, and Ellen White, all of whom left more comfortable situations to take the gospel to faraway places, where customs and sometimes language provided challenges unlike the situation back home.

The shift to postmodern thinking naturally affects the way people approach faith and their relationship to faith-based institutions. The Seventh-day Adventist Church will certainly not be able to continue with business as usual in a postmodern world. I am not suggesting that the church completely discard the fortress model of evangelism. The fortress model worked extremely well in the age of Christian modernism and continues to work well in territories where a large number of Christian modernists can be found, including immigrant cultures in North America, Europe, and Australia. But the increasing impact of secularism and postmodernism on the mainstream cultures of the world can be better met by the incarnational model of outreach.

The salt model points the way to a work for postmoderns that will engage the church and society in a productive interaction. The salt model has the potential to rekindle the fires of outreach that have gone cold in the mainstream cultures of the West. In the process, there is always danger that we will go too far and lose our own faith or get sucked into fruitless and expensive detours. But at the same time, the greater danger is to avoid all change and try to preserve the comfortable and familiar.

So, rather than advocate wholesale change in the face of secular postmodernism, I would suggest nine specific adaptations that can give us a fighting chance to be heard. Each will be somewhat more "radical" than the one before. Every individual, every church, every conference that wants to reach the mainstream culture will need to decide how far it can reasonably go in that endeavor. While some of the nine points are quite radical, they're not just the ravings of a mad mind. Each can be supported by specific scriptures or historical precedent. Each person or entity will need to carefully seek the guidance of the Spirit as it chooses among these principles and applies them.

Let me clarify something once more before I go on. To adopt these nine adaptations does not require abandoning the fortress approach to witnessing. These adaptations are offered as a "salt" option for those to whom God has given a burden to reach postmoderns. The contrasts between a salt approach and a fortress approach should not be seen as a matter of either/or. In most local churches it will be more of a both/and. I emphasize the nine adaptations strongly because they have been neglected in the face of the recent revival of fortress-oriented approaches. Genuine postmoderns are unlikely to respond to settings where none of the following is in place.

## 1. From public to relational evangelism

Traditional Adventist outreach uses public meetings as the crucial factor in spiritual "regime change." But postmoderns are not usually comfortable in that kind of a setting. They are not likely to come to the typical Adventist evangelistic series, nor are they likely to be moved by it if they do come. Experience teaches that postmoderns are best reached one on one, through friendships and mentoring relationships. One-on-one relationships allow people to explore unfamiliar ideas at their own pace in a safe environment. A public meeting can be part of a relational approach, but it will not normally be successful with postmoderns on its own. In working with secular people, Christians should concentrate much more on developing relationships that produce trust than on aggressive approaches that seek immediate decisions. The message of a life in relationship speaks much more loudly than a message delivered only in words.

The relation approach is unquestionably supported by Scripture. Mentoring and discipleship are at the heart of the Great Commission proclaimed by Jesus (see Matthew 28:19, 20). There is only one main verb in the Great Commission, and that verb does not command us to hold public meetings.

It doesn't even command us to teach and baptize. The main verb of the Great Commission is a command to "make disciples." While meetings can be an aid to mentoring relationships, the relationships themselves are the primary evangelistic strategy that Jesus presents in this passage. And it appears to be a strategy that Jesus Himself practiced while He was here on earth, according to Ellen White:

> Christ's method alone will give true success in reaching the people. The Saviour mingled with men as one who desired their good. He showed His sympathy for them, ministered to their needs, and won their confidence. Then He bade them, "Follow Me."
>
> There is need of coming close to the people by personal effort. If less time were given to sermonizing, and more time were spent in personal ministry, greater results would be seen. The poor are to be relieved, the sick cared for, the sorrowing and the bereaved comforted, the ignorant instructed, the inexperienced counseled. We are to weep with those that weep, and rejoice with those that rejoice. Accompanied by the power of persuasion, the power of prayer, the power of the love of God, this work will not, cannot, be without fruit (*The Ministry of Healing*, pp. 143, 144).

## 2. From short term to long term

Traditional Adventist evangelism is usually a short-term project. A local church invests in public meetings, tries to move people to baptism in three to five weeks, and then breathes a sigh of relief for the next year or two. And this strategy can reach people who are at a point of transition, as is the case with most immigrants. But a clear lesson learned from the New York Project in the aftermath of September 11 is that mainstream Americans do not join the Adventist Church in a matter of four to six months, much less four to six weeks. It takes a long-term investment (at least three to five *years*) to make an impact in the mainstream culture.

In the past, Adventists have not shown much patience for this kind of approach. But the model of Jesus' earthly ministry suggests that patience in evangelism should be the norm rather than the exception. Jesus, Himself, the most effective Mentor the world has ever known, invested three and a half years in just twelve people and even then experienced a dropout (Judas). We shouldn't expect things to move more rapidly with postmoderns in today's world.

### 3. From our agenda to felt needs

Traditional Adventist outreach is based on a clear sense of what outsiders need to learn from us. We give it to them the way we think they should hear it, and if they don't get it, that is their "problem." Postmoderns, unfortunately, have proven quite disinterested in our traditional agenda for their souls. They don't feel that the answers we provide are addressing the questions that matter to their lives.

A more successful approach is to listen before we talk. Through listening we can discover the felt needs of the mainstream community and meet them in the power of the gospel. By "felt needs" I don't mean the needs that *we* think they should feel but the needs that *they themselves* feel they have. Paul articulated such a felt-needs approach in 1 Corinthians 9:19–23, suggesting that we should become all things to all people in order to save some.

One major felt need of postmodern secular people is to find a place where they can make a difference in the lives of others. Providing venues where the hungry are fed and the homeless are housed will draw secular people into supporting relationships with Christians. This common mission can create a bond of spiritual fellowship. Churches that are involved in practical ways in their communities will be much more welcoming places for secular people.

Postmoderns want to give not just their dollars but themselves. Short-term missions—both the local and the international variety—can be a powerful draw. Postmoderns love to travel. They love to experience other cultures, and they love to make a difference. All these things can be accomplished by mission trips that bond members and nonmembers together in a shared spiritual experience. As postmoderns see that authentic faith produces genuine service, it confirms the validity of Christian faith for them, and they are likely to explore a deeper relationship with Christ and His people.

These first three principles for reaching secular postmoderns are not really all that radical. They are important components in the "best practices" type of public evangelism, as well. It seems to me that anyone seeking to broaden outreach can implement these without major objections from those who resist change. But the following principles will be more difficult for some to accept.

## 4. From church based to neighborhood/workplace based

In the typical Adventist approach to evangelism, meetings are held at the church building. Even if the meetings begin in a public hall, they are moved as soon as possible to the church. But postmoderns are not likely to come to a church, even if they are interested in the topics being presented. On the other hand, mainstream Americans can be found in every neighborhood and every workplace. Adventists are located in the same neighborhoods and workplaces. To be successful in the Western world, we need to meet people where they are. So, a move toward neighborhood and workplace outreach is a step in the right direction.

Paul endorsed this type of approach when he used his skills as a tent maker to meet the mainstream people of his day. Spending large amounts of time at a tent workshop in the middle of town enabled Paul to meet many people who would never have come to a synagogue. Paul was truly meeting the people where they were. Paul's example as well as the realities of postmodernism suggest that we consider moving from a church-centered mission to a mission-centered church. The church is not so much the *goal* of mission; rather, it is the *instrument* through which the mission can be accomplished.

Neighborhood and workplace outreach require a great deal of creativity. One possibility is affinity groups, where people gather for lunch at the workplace or in someone's home to share a common interest for the environment, family life issues, workplace ethics, or whatever the individuals in the group hold in common. The affinity could even be something like a common interest in football. I once reached a man spiritually by spending a few afternoons watching football with him. Out of relationship came trust, and with trust came a renewed openness for spiritual things.

Currently, my wife and I are moving into a brand-new subdivision in Southern California. It dawned on my wife that one of life's most stressful events is selling a house that you have lived in for years and years. When the first family to express an interest in our house in Michigan asked the price, she broke down and cried. She wasn't ready to put a price on her impending loss. Every room and every mark on the walls contain memories. It dawned on my wife that every woman in our new subdivision will have gone through a similar experience in the months before they moved in to their new house. So, she plans to knock on doors, offer some homemade bread or granola, and invite these women over to our new house to share their experiences. Over time, this may open a window into the spiritual interests of many. Be creative where you are.

## 5. From one way to a multiplicity of approaches

The typical Adventist evangelistic approach does not significantly differ from a model that goes all the way back to an evangelist named Simpson in 1902. Though there are variations, the overall approach is fairly consistent. Those to whom it appeals respond very well, but the percentage of people that find it relevant seems to be declining, at least in the Western world.

Postmoderns are as diverse as snowflakes. The beautiful thing is that such diversity can be countered with the kind of variety bequeathed by the Spirit (see 1 Corinthians 12–14). Truly Spirit-filled Christians do not fit into a cookie-cutter mold either; in fact, they are rather unpredictable, like the wind (see John 3:8). The variety of the Spirit's gifts will lead to a multiplicity of approaches to meet the various mind-sets and felt needs of the postmodern seeker.

The best people to reach out to postmodern secular people will be individuals who have experienced life deeply. They will have suffered from life's troubles. They will have engaged God deeply and personally and come to know who they are in Christ. They will know the purpose of their lives, and their wisdom will shine through in unobtrusive ways. Neighbors and workmates will seek them out as mentors. And they will seek to utilize all the gifts the Spirit has given them to connect with people who will not respond to traditional approaches. Others in the church may criticize their creativity because it doesn't look or feel like "the old-time religion." But people moved by the Spirit will exercise their gifts in the courage that comes with a knowledge of God's approval.

## 6. From a conversion to a process focus

Traditional Adventist evangelism focuses on conversion and baptism. Imagine a continuum that goes from -10 to +10 (see a carefully worked-out example of such a continuum in chapter 14). On one end, -10 designates a person who has absolutely no knowledge of God. On the other, +10 designates a fully devoted follower of God. The zero point is the point of conversion and baptism. Traditional evangelism focuses on getting people from -2 into plus territory. Unless baptisms result, the effort is not considered successful. But mainstream Americans tend to be far deeper into the minus continuum than the typical evangelistic "interest." This means we have little or no impact in the mainstream community.

Salt evangelism, on the other hand, can occur even when there is no immediate baptism in view. If a person moves from -8 to -6 on the scale, successful evangelism has occurred. The key to a focus on process is to encourage the people with whom we are working to begin, or continue, moving in the direction of Jesus. And process evangelism is not limited to reaching secular people. The idea of process is also relevant to the "plus" side of the spectrum, nurturing baptized saints into a more fully devoted discipleship.

The book, *The Desire of Ages,* makes it clear that Jesus was dedicated to process evangelism. The best biblical examples of process are found in the way He handled both Judas and Peter. In both cases the journey was fitful and full of digressions and dead ends. Yet, Jesus continued to work with both of these men and eventually succeeded with Peter. Jesus' patience with long, slow conversions is a good model for working with postmoderns.

I wrote a book—*The Day That Changed the World*—designed to move postmoderns from -8 to -5 or -6 on the continuum. This is challenging to do in the Adventist context. A book that interests postmoderns might not interest the very Adventists you are depending on to distribute it. I have never given *The Day That Changed the World* to someone on an airplane without an enthusiastic response after a few minutes of reading. Yet, the book somehow never came to the attention of the Adventist audience. And it was quickly forgotten.

If we want to make an impact in the mainstream world, we need to write in ways that attract their interest and lead them to spiritual questions. *The Day That Changed the World* (September 11) takes readers from an interest in current events and the war on terror to an inward search for meaning in tragedy. The final destination of the book is the day that truly changed the world—one Friday in Jerusalem. The book invites the reader to investigate the claims of Jesus. A new book that takes a similar approach is *Grounds for Belief,* by my friend Ed Dickerson. He uses the language and the questions of the younger generation to gradually build an interest in what Jesus and faith have to offer. If we want to reach the mainstream, we will need to commit to a process, perhaps a long-term process. And keep in mind the process that God took all of us through in our journey to Him.

These last three principles have been more challenging than the first three. And the last three are more challenging yet. You or your church group may not be ready to consider these as options. And you will certainly not want to go down this path unless God truly guides in that direction. But some will find in the following principles the most basic reasons why we have had so little impact on the new generation so far.

## 7. From church to community

Adventists have grown accustomed to the idea that a community of believers has to meet in a building that is called a "church" and that looks like a church. But postmoderns rarely think of church buildings in positive terms. They tend to think of them as architecturally challenged and a waste of space. Many have unpleasant memories of earlier experiences in a church building, remembering them as either boring or abusive. At some point in their experience they have been burned by the idea of "church."

In Britain and some other places, many postmoderns will cross the street rather than walk by a church. The very style of the church building can be a turnoff. So, an Adventist community that is seriously interested in reaching postmoderns will consider new models for community. Cafés, health centers, gymnasiums, and "house churches" are among the models being tried.

This may seem painfully radical to you—perhaps even heretical. But you might be shocked to find out that the oldest known church building in the Roman world is usually dated somewhere between A.D. 250–300. It is located at Dura-Europus, in Syria. So, for more than two hundred years the early Christian church flourished without church buildings. Our fixation today with such structures is a legacy of Constantine, a character we don't normally take as a model of sound New Testament thinking! In New Testament times, most congregations seem to have met in the largest home available to the members in that area. So, other forms of community are not contrary to Scripture.

Do such ideas spell the death of the traditional congregation? Not at all. For one thing, the global migration of peoples means that most communities in the Western world will have a continual influx of people from a variety of places. These will include Christian moderns as well as secular people. People torn from their roots will look for communities that share a similar faith to the one they knew back home. So, for the foreseeable future there will be a place for the traditional congregation in a traditional church building.

Such congregations can still have an impact on the modern and postmodern secular community to the extent that the members encourage a culture of engagement with the surrounding culture. If a traditional church community has a passion for lost people and is willing to follow God's principles of meeting people where they are, secular people can be reached and incorporated into the community over time. But greater results will occur if secular people can be brought into a community that is sensitive to the needs and expectations of the mainstream culture. Such a community can become the extended family that many secular people have lost. Such a community can provide the intimacy that is so often crowded out of hurried lives in a technological world. Remember that postmoderns, in particular, need to feel that they *belong* before they are willing to explore what they should *believe*.

## 8. From church controlled to God controlled

These kinds of changes are both exciting and scary. Moving to long-term, relational, process-oriented evangelism is challenging enough. If the community is no longer identified with a traditional church building, it moves things even further out of our control. But isn't this what "Let go and let God" is all about? That He, not us, is in control of the spiritual journey? That He is the only One who can safely control the pace and tempo of a person's spiritual growth?

The traditional evangelistic process goes to great pains to track people from first contact through interest to evangelistic series to baptism. This procedure is quite effective with Christian moderns. It will be very hard for the church to give up. Yet, in the long run we may not have a choice. The postmodern conversion process is usually difficult to track and to enumerate. I find it so even with my own children. And in the case of those not brought up in a traditional church, the process will likely include entities not tied to the church or even encounters with other religions.

When dealing with postmoderns it is particularly important to allow them to think for themselves and to grow at their own pace. We need to trust them to the Holy Spirit. Do we trust the Holy Spirit enough to leave them in God's hands? Or do we need to force the issue and try to get a commitment before it is ripe? Can we leave some issues open-ended enough that the glory for conversion goes to God and not to the evangelist or the one doing the witnessing? Churches who measure success primarily on the basis of trackable numbers will not enjoy working for secular people.

It will not be easy for us to give up our control of the conversion process. We may find it hard to trust that God will use our efforts to His glory even if we never see the final outcome of our labors. Paul suggested the biblical model of control when he said, "I planted, Apollos watered, but God gave the increase" (1 Corinthians 3:6, NKJV). Sometimes we will reap a harvest from the work of others. Sometimes others will reap a harvest from our efforts. Perhaps in this generation the concept of "sheep-stealing" will lose its opprobrium and will be recognized as the norm for spiritual growth and development. When the sheep are permitted a choice in the matter, they tend to take a roundabout course.

The beauty of giving up control to God is that it frees us to see His hand in action. As we allow ourselves to depend on Him, He will become more real to us. The path of God control is truly scary, but it is the ultimate antidote to both our personal and corporate selfishness. It will be a path that attracts rather than repels those who are tired of image and corporate selfishness. When others get the credit for our spiritual work, we will be able to say the greatest words ever spoken by a human other than Jesus: " 'He must increase, but I must decrease' " (John 3:30, NKJV).

## 9. From exclusive to inclusive

For more than a decade I have felt that the Seventh-day Adventist Church faces a crisis of identity. On the one hand, many of us want a relatively small, focused, doctrinally pure church with consistent standards of belief and lifestyle. On the other hand, we believe that God wants us to go into the whole world and reach out to all kinds of people. But reaching out to all kinds of different people will require a flexibility and an inclusiveness that will make the first goal rather difficult to attain.

We are facing a tension between exclusiveness and inclusiveness, between a focus on pure teaching and a focus on the openness of grace. If we concentrate on purity, we will become smaller and more idiosyncratic. At its extreme, such an approach would result in a community more like the Amish than the mainstream culture. But if we concentrate on "becoming all things to all people" (see 1 Corinthians 9:22, 23), we may become a great multitude that exhibits a wide variety of worship styles and standards. We may lose our identity in the process of sharing it with others.

It seems to me that, as a group, we have tried to run a route down the middle, thus losing the potential benefits of either approach. Perhaps it is God's ideal to pursue both sides of this seeming dilemma. But if God's hand is truly involved in the emerging postmodern condition, we will need to become more inclusive and open in the way that we deal with others. We may need to give greater attention to Jesus' statement, "he that is not against us is for us" (Luke 9:50, KJV; cf. Mark 9:40).

There is a marvelous Old Testament statement of inclusion in Isaiah 56. This chapter advocates the inclusion of foreigners and eunuchs into the worship at the sanctuary (see verses 3–7). This is a shocking statement within the Old Testament because such inclusion was explicitly forbidden in the laws of Moses. Deuteronomy 23:8 makes it clear that foreigners can be included in worship at the sanctuary only after the third generation. Deuteronomy 23:1 prohibits from worship those whose sexual organs have been mutilated. So, Isaiah goes against the grain, offering "outsiders" full access to the God of Israel. Whatever purpose God had in these exclusions at the time of the Exodus would not apply in the end-time situation described by Isaiah. In a subsequent passage, Isaiah proclaims that some of these foreigners will even be accepted as priests (see Isaiah 66:19–21). In Isaiah, God is redrawing the boundary lines of Israel according to the specifications of His character, not the limits of Israel's vision.

There is a time and a place for exclusion. There is a time and a place for setting boundaries and protecting identities above all else. But there is evidence in Scripture that God's ideal is to move the human race from exclusion to inclusion. There is evidence that the end-time situation will be one in which God will sweep away the barriers and give human beings a fresh glimpse of His redemptive purpose. The main barrier against inclusion is not God's heart but the hearts of human beings. True faithfulness to God will open the way to a breathtaking inclusiveness that will embrace a multitude from every "nation, tribe, language and people" (Revelation 14:6, NIV). In the end, God's house will be " 'a house of prayer for all' " (Isaiah 56:7, NIV; Mark 11:17).

Such a spirit of inclusion will be very encouraging and affirming to postmodern people. In far too many cases, they have been abused and/or neglected by two-income, career-oriented parents. They have experienced similar instances of abuse in the context of religious institutions. They are leery of anyone who says "I am right and you are wrong." Before they will be willing to hear the *challenge* of the gospel, they need to experience the *welcome* of the gospel.

## Conclusion

These nine points set a basic strategy for reaching out to secular people in today's world. The "salt" ministry that is needed is in considerable contrast to the approaches that work best among Christian moderns. As a church, we will need to become more flexible and have the kind of understanding that Paul developed with Peter and James (see Galatians 2:1–10). Recognizing that Jews and Gentiles would not be reached by the same type of approach, Paul and the Jerusalem apostles "shook hands" on an agreement to go separate ways in mission. But the differences between them were not doctrinal; they were for the sake of the mission. Paul and the other apostles agreed on the core of the message. It wasn't what they said that differed but how they said it.

The biggest challenge to implementing a ministry for secular people, whether modern or postmodern, will come from those who are already in the church. They will not oppose out of perversity (in most cases, at least) but out of a concern that the gospel not be compromised. This is a valid concern. Adventures in innovative outreach can lead to fuzzy thinking and confused practice. Those who intend to reach out in radical ways have a responsibility to be accountable to those who know and practice the message. While those who do not embark on innovative journeys may hold back out of fear or cautiousness, they can play a role in keeping the mission on track.

Those involved in "salt" ministry, therefore, will need to stay in touch with less adventuresome colleagues and let them know two things: (1) that they are as passionate about the mission and message of the Seventh-day Adventist Church as those who operate in the "fortress mode" of outreach and (2) that they are not rejecting the fortress. Both salt and fortress approaches are necessary in order to meet people where they are. Those reaching out to secular people need the support and encouragement of the fortress. And they should be willing to offer support and encouragement in return.

## Two Biblical Options for a Postmodern World

| Fortress | Salt | Biblical Basis |
|---|---|---|
| Public | One-to-one/relational | Matthew 28:19, 20 |
| Short term | Long term | Jesus' ministry |
| Our agenda | Felt needs | 1 Corinthians 9:19–23 |
| Church based | Neighborhood/ workplace based | Paul's tent-making |
| One way | Spiritual gift based/ multiplicity of approaches | 1 Corinthians 12–14 |
| Conversion focus | Process focus | Peter, Judas |
| Community as church (church = building) | New models for community (homes, gyms, cafés) | No church buildings until third or fourth century |
| Church controlled | God controlled | 1 Corinthians 3:5–7 |
| Exclusive | Inclusive | Luke 9:50; Mark 9:40 |

# CHAPTER TWELVE

# Meeting Needs Creatively

How can we share our faith in a modern and postmodern secular world? How do we get past the many barriers that secular people erect in order to protect themselves against the unwanted influence of religion? A good place to start is to deal with secular people the same way that Jesus dealt with people. And that is to meet them at the point of felt need, that place in their lives where they are searching for something better than what they have now: "Christ's method alone will give true success in reaching the people. The Saviour mingled with men as one who desired their good. He showed His sympathy for them, ministered to their needs, and won their confidence. Then He bade them, 'Follow Me'" (*The Ministry of Healing*, p. 143).

What is most interesting in this quotation is the fact that apparently Jesus left the direct spiritual appeal to the last in a series of five steps. He spent time with people, (1) "mingling" in conversation, (2) showing sympathy, (3) meeting their needs, and (4) winning their confidence before He (5) challenged them with His unique mission. His method is still the best method.

Note how closely this statement follows the salt side of the chart on page 134. Jesus worked for people one on one in the neighborhoods and workplaces where they could be found. His approach was not a short-term approach. He invested more than three years in a handful of disciples, and most of them didn't "get it" until after His death and resurrection. Jesus' approach was centered on people's needs and was therefore individualized to meet them where they were. Christ's method outlines a process. The goal is in mind, but there are many steps along the way. And Jesus was certainly one of the most inclusive people that ever walked this earth.

## The basic needs of secular people

Are there some basic needs that both modern and postmodern seculars have in common? Needs that come close to a direct spiritual interest? Needs that provide potential openings for spiritual input? If so, such needs would be the key starting points in relational outreach.

At this point, it would be helpful to read chapter 16 on the stages of friendship. The summary there gives a brief overview of various levels of friendship, from the most basic acquaintance to the deepest level of intimacy. Most mainstream people consider a spiritual approach at the acquaintance level of relationship to be inappropriate. It is an infringement on their right to space. It is a one-sided projection of a relationship into areas of discussion that are usually reserved for more intimate friends. By knowing the stages of friendship, we can better understand when a secular person will be ready for a deeper and more probing exploration of their inner world. Move too soon or too aggressively and you can set the relationship back for months or even years.

I know that many Christian witnesses use in-your-face approaches with strangers and that there are many anecdotes of how such approaches have led to conversions. The larger the number of people approached in this way, the greater the likelihood that one will "luck into" a person who is receptive to just such an approach at that moment. I have personally experienced occasions when the moving of the Holy Spirit brought me into fruitful spiritual contact with a stranger on the spur of the moment. So, we need to be ready at all times with a witness that seizes the golden moments the Spirit may offer.

But I wonder if in-your-face witnesses have considered the negative consequences of such an indiscriminate approach in the secular environment. Approaching a hundred individuals on the street may produce one or even five spiritual interests, but what is the impact on the others? Has their resistance to spiritual things been strengthened? Has their distaste for "religion" been confirmed? Will there be ninety-nine (or ninety-five) new workplace anecdotes about the cluelessness of Christians and the irrelevance of the gospel? Salt ministry is not only concerned with individual response but with the overall attitudes toward the gospel in the community. The "image" of the gospel is an important concern when working for the secular mainstream.

The quotation above from *The Ministry of Healing* indicates that Jesus did not generally use the in-your-face approach, although He was certainly capable of it (see Matthew 23, for example)! Jesus took time to cultivate relationships by mingling with people, inquiring about their needs and concerns, and gaining their confidence before He moved into a direct spiritual approach. To bypass the natural development of a relationship, unless overwhelmingly directed by the Spirit, will normally do more harm than good. As a preparation for what follows, then, it would be helpful to better understand the stages of relationship and how this may affect the timing of spiritual contact with secular people (see chapter 16).

All of us, Christians and secularists, have a multitude of surface relationships—people we meet regularly on the subway or the bus, people on the job that we encounter occasionally rather than every day, most of our neighbors in those faceless housing developments that so characterize the mainstream Western world, etc. Over time, we discover that some of these acquaintances are curious about the same kinds of things we are. They may be attractive or interesting in some special way. With such individuals we often enter into a "dance" of give and take, exploring whether deeper relationship would be mutually agreeable. If both sides find it agreeable, the relationship can go deeper and reach levels where spiritual needs can be brought up without jeopardizing the relationship. To have a spiritual impact on people in the secular mainstream, it is necessary to go deeper than just the surface. The spiritual side of life cannot be the only interest you have in common with each other.

When that moment comes, there are a number of general felt needs that are fairly common among both modern and postmodern people. I have listed the general needs that come closest to spiritual interest. In addition to these, most individuals will have more specific felt needs that can be determined only by extended contact. But these more general needs provide a good starting point for spiritual contact with those in the Western mainstream. You will notice that Adventism is well placed to meet many of these needs.

## 1. A need for commitment

Secular people generally feel a need for commitment to an issue, a group, or a person that is greater than themselves. People cannot be fully satisfied with an endless round of routine tasks. Meaning must come from outside the ordinary. People may seek to meet that need by a commitment to the Los Angeles Lakers or the Washington Redskins. The fate of a sports team may seem rather trivial as the center of one's life. However, such attachments function as symbols of a far more significant need—the need to be committed to something that is bigger than oneself. The roar of the crowd and rooting for the team feeds a deep and passionate need.

Less trivial substitutes for faith include patriotism and a passion for preserving the environment. More and more people are committing themselves to recycling and reducing consumption so as not to overburden the earth's ecosystem. Protecting our planet is certainly a major and worthy concern. Yet, at the deepest level, I believe that people are searching for something bigger than ecology.

Adventism is uniquely positioned to make a difference here. Our worldview includes the greatest Person and the greatest issues that anyone could possibly commit themselves to. The environment of the entire universe for all eternity is at stake in the work of the gospel. Adventist outreach can provide the grandest of all perspectives, but it will not be easy.

Postmodernism has a strong suspicion of the "biggest ideas." Therefore, we need to learn how to connect the issues of the great-controversy theme to the kinds of issues that secular people take seriously on a day-to-day basis. People will take us seriously on the mega-issues if we can demonstrate that our worldview produces positive change in terms of the mini-issues that people wrestle with every day. Postmodern secular people, in particular, are hungry for practical truth, but impatient with theoretical, abstract constructions. The great-controversy theme will be plausible to the extent that it changes the world in the realm of everyday experience.

## 2. Release from guilt

Although secular people may feel uncomfortable with the term *guilt* in light of its Judeo-Christian associations, they live under the burden of failing to live up to their own expectations. Many no longer take the Ten Commandments seriously, but they have a sense that they don't live up even to what they expect from themselves, much less to the standards that might be held up to them from outside. Even nonreligious people need release from a sense of failure—the failure to achieve their hopes, their dreams, and their best intentions.

It is a fact of life that we inwardly expect of ourselves at least as much as we expect of others. If I point my finger at you and say "You shouldn't do that," what am I saying to myself? *Well, if I can criticize others on this point, it certainly isn't right for me either.* Secular people often have a very strong sense of obligation, a strong sense of where they want to be in life. Failure to achieve those expectations leaves a sense of brokenness that cries out to be fixed. Many may deny that brokenness or drown it in alcohol, drugs, or promiscuity, but it can be fixed ultimately only by the gospel.

So, here is a place where secular people are wide open to the genuine gospel of Jesus Christ, if it comes to them in a living and understandable way. If we are to meet this need, Adventists need to truly understand and appreciate the gospel of Jesus Christ, first of all, for ourselves. Until we do, we cannot meet this deep need that all human beings have, not just secular people. We cannot bring healing to modern and postmodern people if we don't understand how to find that healing for ourselves. I have outlined a relevant approach to the gospel in the books *Knowing God in the Real World* and *Meet God Again for the First Time.*

## 3. Genuine relationships

Secular people today have an urgent need for genuine relationships. They long for real relationships with real people who care enough to be honest as well as loyal. People today live noisy and distracted lives. They are rushing here and there, and relationships tend to be increasingly superficial. A committed Christian who is willing to enter into sensitive and authentic relationships with secular people will find open arms waiting.

The church has a tremendous opportunity here to reach out to struggling, hurting, secular people. Many have avoided church because of the perception that church people are inauthentic and superficial and thus incapable of meeting their deep relational needs. But as a high-tech society makes it more difficult to maintain meaningful relationships, people are becoming open to a wider variety of options in their search for that kind of connection.

One of the reasons people in the Western mainstream are so hungry for relationship is the loss of the extended family. For most of human history,

several generations of a family—along with cousins, aunts, and neph-
ews—all lived in the same community and shared relationships at special
occasions on a regular basis. But these days brothers and sisters, parents
and grandparents, are scattered all over the country, often all over the
world. North American life is increasingly transient, with people moving
wherever jobs or housing opportunities may take them.

But all this opens up special opportunities. Every year, more than a
million new homes are built in preplanned subdivisions. Every person
who moves into such a subdivision has torn themselves away from a prior
home and the relationships available in the previous community. These
new subdivisions may be exciting and fresh, but they are filled with people
who are lonely as a result of their move. Believers moving into such a new
community have a golden (and fairly short-term) opportunity to provide
a sense of extended family for those torn away from their own families of
birth. The Holy Spirit can use our caring touch to activate the need for the
kind of relationship that only God can provide.

## 4. Cosmic philosophy

Secular people have a need for a cosmic philosophy, although postmoderns, in particular, despair that this is possible. Most human beings
long to know that everything somehow fits together, that they belong to a
meaningful and ordered universe. Adventists may not be conscious of this
need because our awareness of cosmic issues in the universe is something
that we often take for granted. Just think what life would be like if you had
no idea where this world came from, no idea how it is going to end, no
idea what the universe beyond the telescope is like.

For Adventists, the whole great controversy scheme is a great organiz-
ing principle for a personal concept of the universe and our place in that
universe. The average person looks out at the sky and has little or no idea
what is going on out there. It is an empty void. All that is known is what
can be perceived on earth by means of the five senses. What we call "escha-
tology" or last-day events—a cosmic philosophy that brings the whole
universe into the equation—is foreign to most people.

At appropriate times, therefore, this sense of place in the larger scheme
of things can be quite meaningful in a secular context. Given what we
have earlier learned about meta-narratives, this is one need more easily
filled for modern secular people than for postmodern secular people.

Modern secularists may not have a God-based big picture of the universe, but they still believe one is possible. Postmoderns find the very concept of a cosmic philosophy challenging, even though deep in their hearts they long for one.

## 5. Lifestyle direction

These days, secular people are earnestly seeking direction for their life-styles. The best-selling book category today is self-help—self-help for plumbing, self-help for home repairs, self-help for marriage, self-help for potty training, etc. The big concern of most young people today is that they do not know what to do with their lives. There is an openness to help from any direction, provided it directly touches felt needs and speaks a language that is familiar and meaningful.

Frankly, no faith anywhere offers more direction for a person's lifestyle than does the Adventist faith. We don't always present the Adventist life-style in a way that meets people where they are, but a lifestyle that "works" is very attractive in the secular context. It needs to come to people from a principled and logical perspective rather than as a set of rigid rules. The secular mainstream is on notice that the Adventist community in Loma Linda, California, may be the longest-lived community on earth (see *National Geographic,* November 2005, for example). There is an interest in the principles that make for a lengthy and successful life. We have a ways to go in communicating this lifestyle effectively, but the opportunity is there.

## Summary

This brief look at some of the basic felt needs of secular people indicates that Seventh-day Adventists have a marvelous opportunity to make major inroads into the secular community. In three of the five areas, we have a contribution to make that exceeds, in some ways, that of any other Chris-tian group. The best approach for Adventists who want to reach secular people would be to aim at their felt needs in the area of lifestyle, with par-ticular emphasis on health, stress management, personal finance, and time management.

We also have a unique niche in the way we integrate lifestyle details into a comprehensive worldview that can provide meaning to every area of people's lives. This has been the strength of Adventism in each previous generation. We have a unified message with a unified worldview. If we can learn to express our convictions in up-to-date language, we may be surprised at the kind of people who will be anxious to become involved.

## The right kind of witness

It clearly takes a special kind of person to reach out to secular people without crossing the barriers of social propriety. It takes what I call a "two-horizon" person, someone who not only is comfortable in a traditional Adventist setting but who can also step out and be comfortable in the secular world. If you intend to bring secular people into community with traditional Adventist people, you will need a deep sensitivity to both groups in order to make it work.

There are at least four qualities that equip an Adventist to expand his or her horizon into the world of modern and postmodern secular people. Most Adventists will not be proficient in all four of these qualities at first, but it is possible for each of us to improve our skills in each of these areas. The more skilled the one witnessing, the more effective the witness.

## Identify with people

The first quality of a good witness to secular people is the ability to rapidly identify with others, to sense where they are coming from. People with this quality have an uncanny ability to speed the process of relationship building. They are able to get close to others in a hurry, to intuitively put themselves in other people's shoes and see the world through their eyes.

In an earlier book, I told the story of Joe, a fellow pastor in the same conference in which I worked. I always envied Joe's razor-sharp ability to zero in on a person and identify what was going on deep inside. I will never forget the time we were both assigned to the paint crew at the conference camp. One Sunday, a number of church members came out to help us for a day. Around ten o'clock a young man was dropped off at our work site with the message, "He's here to help out."

Joe immediately said, "Hi! My name's Joe." He quickly found out that the young man had just come from Eastern Europe.

"Oh," Joe said, "are you here with your family?"

"No, no. My sister's still back there."

Joe took a step closer, looked the young man directly in the eye, and said, "You're worried about your sister, aren't you?"

Immediately, a tear began running down the fellow's cheek. Joe continued, "Why don't we pray about her right now?"

We all dropped to our knees on the paint-stained drop cloth and prayed for this guy's sister. And he hadn't been in the room even five minutes! I continue to find inspiration in Joe's ability to rapidly identify with people.

If you realize, as I do, that you have difficulty identifying with people, take it to the Lord. The Spirit can provide the gifts we need to enhance our ministry to others. But even those who do not feel gifted in this area can learn to identify with people more effectively. All it takes is a little training and practice. Make it a project to learn from your mistakes. The neat thing about postmoderns is that they are very forgiving of relational mistakes— *if* you are honest and genuine. They are usually quite willing to teach you how to talk to them if you give them an honest effort.

As I have repeatedly pointed out, secular ministry is not for everybody. But if you are reading this book, you likely feel God is calling you to make a difference in the secular environment. The best place to start is to sharpen your ability to identify with people and understand the inner drives that motivate their behavior.

## Creative witness

The second quality that sets two-horizon people apart is the ability to offer a fresh and creative witness when the circumstances demand it. A canned or prepackaged approach is limited in its impact to those few who are interested in what that particular kind of can contains. With secular people, it is necessary to "wing it" a lot more than most of us are accustomed to. Fresh and creative witness means the ability to say something that you have never said before because a particular situation requires it. Obviously, the only way we can do this is to be sensitive to the leading of the Holy Spirit. The Spirit can impress you with the right words at the right time just as He did with Jesus while He was here on earth.

I remember visiting a man who claimed to be an atheist. I will call him Zack. According to Zack, the reason he could not believe in God was all the questions no one could answer for him. He began tossing question after question at me. A friend and I took it upon ourselves to answer as many of his questions as we could, yet nothing seemed to satisfy Zack.

Many of his questions seemed rather trivial. Something about this situation didn't click for me. Whenever my friend was speaking, I was pleading with God to help me find some way to reach this man.

Then I felt a strong impression from the Holy Spirit to do something I had never done before. Although I had known this man less than half an hour, I challenged him with painful directness. "You know what interests me most about your questions?" I asked.

"No, what?"

"I don't have answers for many of these questions, yet it doesn't bother me that I don't know. Why does it bother you so much?"

"You tell me," said Zack.

"Well, it seems to me that even if I answered all of your questions today, you would have a hundred more tomorrow. And the next day and the next."

"So?"

"I don't think the questions are the real issue. They are a way of keeping us away from the real issue."

"So, what do you think the real issue is?" Zack said warily.

"In my experience, when a man asks question after question like this, it's because at some time in the past he has had a moral problem, and he has never dealt with it."

Zack looked like a deer caught in the headlights. He was silent for what seemed like two minutes. His wife was sitting behind him, where he couldn't see her. She was nodding her head vigorously, agreeing with me.

After a period of silence, Zack said, "I need to think about that."

After some further silence, he repeated, "I'm going to think about what you said."

The conversation went in other directions before we left, but there were no more questions from Zack. He was fairly quiet the rest of the time. On our way to the car, he pulled me aside and assured me, "I'm really gonna think about what you said."

I rarely nail it like that. And that was certainly a risky approach. I'm tempted to say, "Don't try this at home," except that I know the Spirit was with me on that occasion. With a canned approach to Zack's questions we would have gotten nowhere. Zack would never have opened up to his deepest need. If the Spirit is with you and your heart is sensitive to people, you can often sense the right word at the right time, even when you don't know the people very well. I think that is the way Jesus would have handled the situation. Fresh and creative witness means a willingness to approach people and issues from an entirely different angle than you have ever tried before.

## Biblical knowledge

A third quality essential for those reaching out to secular people is to know the Bible well. I don't mean knowing a series of lessons *about* the Bible but to know the Bible itself well. To know the stories. To know how one idea flows into another. To have a sense of the differences between Matthew, Mark, and Luke. This kind of Bible knowledge certainly does not happen overnight. But a thorough knowledge of the content of the Bible is critical when working with secular people. They almost never ask the questions that are found in the typical set of Bible lessons. They ask questions you have never dreamed of.

Most of our traditional Adventist Bible lessons were designed to persuade people who already know Christ and are familiar with their Bibles. Secular people find it difficult to relate to that kind of biblical knowledge. To know the Bible well is to be prepared for off-the-wall questions. The goal at such times is to reorient your biblical knowledge and provide an answer from Scripture that transcends anything you knew before the question came.

This may seem an impossible task at first, but you must not allow the enormity of the task to slow you down. If you have no idea how to answer, just say, "That's a great question! Hey, do you mind if I go home and think about it for a while? A question as good as that deserves a solid answer. Give me a little time, and I'll get back to you." Secular people don't expect you to have all the answers at the tip of your fingers. In fact, they may be turned off if you imply that you do!

My favorite style of evangelism is what I call "open forum." Open forum style permits people to interrupt anytime to ask questions or offer comments. It is a lot like some of the talk shows on television. Secular people find the open forum style entertaining as well as challenging. The give and take of intellectual debate attracts people's interest. The challenge of open forum, of course, is that you never know what you are going to face, so you had better know your Bible and be sensitive to the Spirit's guidance.

Do you need a Ph.D. in biblical studies to reach secular people? No. The key is simply to spend a lot of time with the Bible. And I don't mean reading books about the Bible or studying Bible lessons. I really mean *studying the Bible* itself. Spend more time reading the Bible than you spend perusing a concordance or helps. The broader your knowledge of the Bible's big picture, the more able you will become to apply the Bible authentically to any and every situation.

## Common language

The fourth quality of a good "witness" to secular people is the use of basic, everyday language in presenting the gospel. There is a language that is common to everyone who speaks English—the kind of language used in magazines like *Newsweek* or on the typical Web site. These media utilize a basic eight thousand to ten thousand word vocabulary that communicates to virtually everyone. We Adventists, on the other hand, often use our own "in-house" language, which communicates accurately only among us.

Adventists who are educated and who work in white-collar jobs know how to talk to secular people on a day-to-day basis. But we tend to reserve that language for the secular part of our lives and switch to a different language when we want to express our spiritual needs and concerns. We describe our walk with God in terms like "justification" and "sanctification." We have "seen the light." We know about the "close of probation" and the "time of trouble."

All of these concepts are useful and important. But they make no sense to someone raised outside of Adventism. In order for Adventism to connect with modern and postmodern secular people, it needs to be "translated" into everyday English. This is not easy. We need to challenge each other to express spiritual feelings in everyday language even within the church. That way it will already be second nature when we reach outside to others.

As a pastor in New York City, one of the intellectual capitals of the secular world, I went out of my way to screen my sermons with this need in mind. I would ask myself at every step of preparation, "What sense would this language make to somebody coming in off the street? How can I make it as basic and clear as possible without muddying the content?" I gradually learned that I could talk about complex things without using complex language. It takes time to learn to do this.

I remember with much regret the time I learned a particular couple was coming to my church on Sabbath. I prepared a sermon "just for them." I hadn't reached the ten minute mark before I realized that nothing I was saying would connect with them. I had totally blown it, but I didn't know what to do to redeem the situation. They never came back. It took years for me to learn to use common language, and then it took a few more years to start overcoming the impact of Ph.D. studies on my vocabulary. The more we learn to use common, everyday language, the wider the impact we can make on a diverse audience.

## Conclusion

The basic principle of all gospel outreach is meeting people where they are. In order to do that with secular people, you have to begin by learning all you can about their general needs and interests. That will give you a good starting point for discovering the needs of specific secular individuals.

The second key is to be the kind of person they will want to be reached by! The four qualities described briefly above are basic to that personal profile. They require both involvement with the Holy Spirit and much effort and experience. It's not necessary, however, to master all these areas before you can begin reaching out to secular people.

The good news is that God enables those whom He calls. If you feel called to develop an outreach to modern or postmodern people, I invite you to commit yourself before God to get the training and experience that will make a difference in the quality of your efforts. The very best training, however, lies in actually reaching out to secular people. How to begin doing that is the topic of the next chapter.

# CHAPTER THIRTEEN

# Reaching Out One to One

The preceding chapter concluded with a sobering reality. The greatest Adventist shortcoming in dealing with secular people may be our failure to apply everyday language to matters of faith. This may seem puzzling at first glance, since we may both be speaking English, Spanish, or German. But the way secular people use language and the kinds of questions they ask are radically different than the kinds of things Adventists talk about among themselves. Unless major efforts are made, the gulf between the Adventist way of speaking and thinking and that of the Western mainstream is not easily bridged.

So, if we want to move from theory to practice and actually connect with secular people, we will need to learn a whole new language. We will need to understand the way they think, the things that trouble them, and the needs that drive their search for something better in their lives. How do we do that in practical terms? The same way children learn language, by listening and talking. If we never interact with secular people, we will never truly learn how to reach them with the gospel. But as we interact regularly with secular people over time, we will gradually learn how to communicate effectively with them.

## Creative listening

What is the best way to get close to secular people? Creative listening. Creative listening is the art of asking leading questions, questions that gently zero in on what really matters in the other person's life. Creative listening doesn't come naturally for me. I tend to talk too much and listen too little. A willingness to listen is fundamental.

But listening must be more than an idle task if it is to be constructive. If you simply sit back and let a secular person wander wherever he will, you will hear a lot of nonsense, a lot of unprocessed experience, and sometimes a whole lot of foul language. Allowing a person to wander wherever he wants results in what some call a "stream of consciousness." Stream of consciousness has even become something of an art form in the postmodern world, as evidenced by the short vignettes of MTV and YouTube. So, unless one gives a conversation some direction, most people today will wander all over the place and not even realize that the conversation is going nowhere.

An interesting illustration of creative listening can be found in Ellen White's description of Jesus' conversation with the Samaritan woman (see *The Desire of Ages,* pp. 184–190). At one point in the conversation Jesus lets her carry the discussion "whither she would" (p. 188). When Jesus zeros in on her marital relationships, she tries to distract Him by wandering off into a theological discussion. At another point He abruptly changes the subject Himself (see p. 187). The point is that Jesus had a purpose for the conversation, even when He allowed the woman to express a little "stream of consciousness." Creative listening is more proactive than reactive. The goal of creative listening is much more than just passing the time.

Creative listening aims to discover the felt needs that drive another person's life. It means asking questions that sensitively encourage another person to reveal those things that are of central concern in his life. My friend Joe was extremely effective at this. He rarely needed more than five questions before he discovered the central area of need in someone's life. I wish I were equally gifted in this area.

Creative listening means learning to ask the right question at the right time. Most people love to talk about themselves, and they love others who are good listeners. Through questions we invite a secular person to talk about his or her family, job, hopes, and dreams. As the relationship deepens, we can also ask about his fears and worries. We allow him to unpack his emotional life. These questions provide a relaxed and nonthreatening way to guide the conversation in constructive directions.

Creative listening can be challenging. Most people are naturally reluctant to overstep the comfort zone of others. Will you make mistakes when you listen? Will you overstep people's boundaries and embarrass yourself from time to time? Of course. But there is no better way to learn how to talk to the secular mainstream than to actually try doing it. There are a couple of keys, however, that can minimize our mistakes as we explore new relationships.

First, we can be attentive to the stages of friendship (see chapter 16). There is a sense in which creative listening is all about being a good friend. A good friend is a good listener. A good friend will not push a relationship faster than it should grow. When a relationship is at Stage 2 (facts and reports), for example, we do not force the other person to talk about his feelings (Stage 4), unless there is a context for that, such as a death in the family or a sick child. A good friend is attentive to where the relationship is at any moment.

Second, we will have few problems with creative listening if we ourselves are open and honest. As we have noted, both modern and postmodern people are hungry for genuine relationships. A person who is willing to talk about his or her own feelings (Stage 4) and failures (Stage 5) leaves the way open to deeper relationship. The other person can "decline the offer" and leave the relationship at Stage 2 or Stage 3. If he does that, give him space. But most secular people will seize the opportunity to go past the surface. And you have made a new friend. You will know creative listening is working when more than one secular person announces to others that you are his best friend!

Even if you're naturally shy, you don't need to fear this process. Secular people are usually forgiving of relational mistakes, if the other person is reasonably honest and open. If you make a relational mistake just say, "Oh, I think that was the wrong thing to say." Or "Sorry, I blew that one." As long as we don't wear our feelings on our sleeve, communicating with secular people will be a great adventure.

Someone may object, "Didn't Jesus zero in right to the point with the rich young ruler? He didn't waste time with a lot of fancy listening."

It's true that Jesus often went right to the heart of an issue. The difference between Jesus and me, however, is that Jesus could read the heart (see John 2:23–25) much better than I can. For me to be as direct as Jesus sometimes was, I will need to go through a lengthy two-step process. First, I must remove any barriers that may prevent His Spirit from impressing me regarding others. Second, I need to spend a lot of time in creative listening. I can't understand most strangers without much listening first.

Although the Spirit will sometimes speed up the process of relationship building, God doesn't normally choose to bypass the human process of learning. If it were better in the ultimate scheme of things for angels or the Spirit to do the work of outreach, they would gladly do it. But God has chosen to give this task to us. Why? Because as we go through the laborious process of listening to secular people, we will learn lessons about ourselves that we could learn no other way. And He has entrusted this task to us also because creative listening is a marvelous way to demonstrate Christlike love. Notice the words of John Stott: "Dialogue is a token of genuine Christian love, because it indicates our steadfast resolve to rid our minds of the prejudices and caricatures which we may entertain about other people; the struggle to listen through their ears and look through their eyes so as to grasp what prevents them from hearing the gospel and seeing Christ, to sympathize with them in all their doubts, fears and hangups."[*]

As any successfully married couple knows, love and listening are two sides of the same coin. Our strategizing, therefore, must never take the place of a genuine love for lost people. In a postmodern world, any outreach that is motivated by money, reputation, or institution building is doomed to failure. It is not enough to have the right *strategy* for reaching secular people. All we do must be grounded and motivated by a genuine love. This will not happen outside of our relationship with God. It is God who can bypass our natural selfishness and fill our hearts with love for secular people. When we have that kind of love, strategy can channel that love in effective ways.

## The point of contact

Creative listening in love, therefore, is the starting point for outreach to a secular world. Through attentive listening and an awareness of how friendships develop, we can get close to secular people. This is the method of Jesus who "mingled with others as one who desired their good." Friendships grow and develop when both parties feel there is something to be

---

[*] Quoted in James F. Engel, *Contemporary Christian Communications: Its Theory and Practice* (Nashville: Thomas Nelson, 1979), 60.

gained from the relationship. But what is the goal of this relationship building from an outreach perspective?

The goal is to discover the felt needs that open a person to input from others. What are the basic needs that motivate that person's search for truth and self-betterment? Where is that person hurting at the moment? What are the current problems in their lives that stimulate a desire for something better?

Of course, there can be a difference between genuine needs and felt needs. Every person has needs that he or she is not aware of. And the greatest of all human needs is to know Christ. But most people aren't aware of their need for Christ, and they would deny their need for the gospel. So, the starting point must be to aim at their felt needs.

As noted in the first chapter, *every human being has a built-in barrier against persuasion.* Human beings have a natural aversion to changing their minds. And it is a good aversion. If we didn't have it, we would all change religions every day. We would all believe the very last thing we were told about God. There are people who were born and raised without a very strong barrier against persuasion. Perhaps you have met some. They jump from one idea to the next and never quite settle on anything. They are known as credulous or easily duped.

However, most people have a strong barrier against persuasion. They don't lightly change their minds on any topic. When somebody comes along with an idea that is radically different than what they believe, a psychological brick wall goes up. And the more you pound against that wall, the more it is reinforced. But there is a way around those walls. The way around is to approach people in the area of their felt needs. A felt need is a point in a person's life when they are open to instruction. Students of world mission call this felt need the point of contact, that point in a person's or a group's experience when an aspect of the gospel intersects with conscious needs and interests.

This felt-need principle, however, introduces some complexity into the outreach process, because secular people are diverse. If you talk to ten secular individuals, you may discover ten completely different felt needs, none of which you have ever met in quite that form before. Without a fresh and creative approach, the situation may appear hopeless. But although the attempt will have its ups and downs, it is a great adventure that will enrich the life of everyone who thrives on adventure.

## Door-to-door listening

How do you put the felt-need principle to work on a large scale, such as a church outreach ministry? The most basic strategy is listening to the community you are planning to reach. It is helpful to begin such listening with demographic studies. Put some of your teens to work on the Internet, searching out all the information they can about your target audience, whether that is a particular neighborhood, ethnic group, or age segment (such as young adults or seniors). You can also talk to your pastor or conference leadership about marketing studies related to specific zip codes. These studies give you an idea of how well a particular community responds to Adventist outreach. Or you can contact the Institute of Church Ministry at Andrews University for assistance.

The general information available through demographic studies can become the basis for the next step, which I call door-to-door listening. Based on what your church group learns about your target audience, create a short survey that attempts to discover more specific and detailed felt needs that are common in the target community. As early returns from the survey come in, it is important to modify the survey itself on the basis of the feedback. As areas of interest emerge, the local church or group can assess which of these felt needs it is in a position to address. The ideal outreach plan will develop at the intersection of community need and the church's ability to meet that need.

Let me give you an example. I spent a weekend with a large, hospital-based church in an upscale university town. After covering some of the principles in this book, we had a brainstorming session in which the leaders of the church compared what they knew of community needs with the skills and gifts the church had available. The church had a large number of medical professionals. After considering the gifts and interests of the church members, it was concluded that the ideal outreach for that church would be a vegetarian restaurant along the walking mall at the center of that university town.

The next day I took a walk in that mall and found two vegetarian restaurants already there (one had Indian food and the theme of the other could be characterized as "New Age spirituality"). I suggested that the community's felt need for vegetarian food was probably being fairly well satisfied. The church then explored other possible areas where the church's gifts and the community's needs intersected. One area that emerged was a need for affordable health care for students. Could the church put together a wellness program for the students on the university campus? The best outreach to the secular mainstream will arise at the intersection between community needs and the gifts of the church.

In an inner-city area of Milwaukee, young people ten to twenty years of age had nothing to do outside of school hours. An Adventist elementary school was located smack in the center of that neighborhood and was completely locked up and barred (understandably) after school hours. (The students in the school mostly commuted in from other neighborhoods.) Several young adults had a burden for the youth of that neighborhood. Being interested in sports themselves, they petitioned the churches responsible for the school to allow them to offer recreational activities in the school gym several evenings a week. This outreach has gone on for several years now. Recently, a new youth pastor in the area held meetings for the youth who were coming to the gym. As I write, more than twenty of these kids are preparing for baptism, and their families are being included in the studies. The most effective outreach comes at the intersection of community need and the church's ability to meet that need.

What if you live in an urban area with high-rise buildings which don't allow access to the public? You can still get a lot of feedback if empathetic people with a strong desire to improve the community reach out to people where they work, shop, or relax. Here's another example. A group of us once reached out to a troubled community in the South Bronx. At the time, the South Bronx looked like Berlin in 1945. There was garbage in the street, broken glass in the empty lots, burned-out buildings, and a few high-rises that were hanging together by a thread. It didn't look promising.

It was a bright, sunny day, and lots of people were sitting on stoops and standing in clumps along the street. A group of us went through the neighborhood talking to the people about the felt needs of that community. The author of the questionnaire had developed an interesting set of questions including, "Do you feel good about the condition of this block?" In answer to this question, 100 percent of the people said "No." They did not feel good about the way the neighborhood was. The next question was, "If someone would take the lead in cleaning up this block, would you help?" To my amazement, 90 percent said "Yes" in an area known for apathy.

Was that block begging for an evangelistic campaign? Or was it an opportunity for a person with a Christlike heart to move into that block and get involved in the neighborhood? Such a person could encourage the people to galvanize their resources to clean up the empty lot, to plant flowers, to provide security, etc. It could be done. Most people are afraid to take the lead. But if someone leads out, others will follow. To meet a felt need like this would create a great deal of interest in whatever else the church has to offer.

Buchanan, Michigan, is a more traditional type of neighborhood with single-family houses and small yards. Traditional door-to-door work is possible there. I supervised a group of seminary students who knocked on doors and administered a survey to determine community felt needs. The cumulative results of the survey told us that the Buchanan community had three outstanding felt needs—stress, personal and family finance, and, like Milwaukee, activities for young people, especially in the summer. Our church felt it had the resources to offer stress and financial seminars and to provide a high-quality Vacation Bible School for the community. All these programs attracted good crowds.

After listening to the community, therefore, it is helpful to survey the church to find out what resources and interests are available. The neighborhood survey indicates where the "fertile fields" are; it identifies people and groups who are open in specific areas of need. And when felt needs emerge, the Spirit will move on the hearts of believers to take action! Either they will have the gifts that are needed or God will help them find people with those gifts.

There is one further way of listening to the community besides demographics, surveys, and personal friendships. It can be tremendously helpful to get acquainted with the "movers and shakers" in a community. Whether the community is large or small, there are local leaders that have their fingers on its pulse. They include the mayor of a small town or the supervisor of a township or urban neighborhood. They include the principals of the public and private schools and the chief of police or the head of the local police precinct. A look at local newspapers will bring out other influential individuals, from columnists to sports coaches to medical professionals to business people. A pastor or influential lay person would be the ideal person to get interviews with such people and get an educated sense of what makes a particular community tick.

The more you know about the felt needs of people and of communities, the more accurate will be the church's response to the mainstream culture. We have to learn before we can earn the right to teach.

## Kindness ministries

One further strategy that can help put Adventist people in contact with the modern and postmodern mainstream of a community is "kindness ministries." In a world that is saturated with advertising, people feel a bit suspicious toward outreach of any kind. They are always wondering what the "catch" is, what the person offering a service is getting out of it. Out of love for lost people, many churches are catching a vision of kindness, offering benefits to the community without any catch. Ellen White called this "disinterested benevolence." We benefit the community, not to add to the church's numbers or influence, but simply because it is the right thing to do. In the postmodern context, this is more important than ever.

I remember a time when my church in New York City was caroling to raise funds for world missions and also for local services in the areas of nutrition, health, and stress management. I was driving the car that broadcasted Christmas music as a background for members who were knocking on doors and inviting people to contribute. Every so often I would leave the car running and go to a door or two myself.

On this particular evening we were passing through what I would characterize as an "upper-middle-class neighborhood." The rows of houses were very nice. At one of these doors a middle-aged man was furious at our "intrusion." He told me what he thought of money-grubbing churches and charities and in no uncertain terms said that he was much too poor to contribute anything.

I resisted the opportunity to point out that he was far better off than the starving children pictured on the brochure we were handing out. Instead, I opened the brochure and pointed out the insert which described the many classes and services our churches were providing in his community. "I'm sorry to hear things aren't going well for you," I said. "That's why we offer the programs that we do. Why don't you look through this brochure? Maybe there is something we offer that can help *you.*"

I left him at the door and went back to the car. Several minutes later he came looking for me in the street. He apologized for his behavior and handed me several dollars. "I looked through the brochure. You're doing a good work," he said.

Sometimes Adventist churches don't have the best reputation in the mainstream community. This can be for any number of reasons. A good way to turn around that situation is a kindness ministry. A kindness ministry offers something a community needs without any strings attached. It could be tutoring children at a local school. It could be offering rides to shut-ins who have no car. It could be providing packets of sunscreen to people watching a Fourth of July parade in the hot sun. It could be providing cool drinks to runners at a marathon.

Kindness ministries don't require extensive training or specialized skills. Anyone can be involved; all you need is a desire to do something nice for other people. Kindness ministries build enthusiasm, energy, and a sense of mission among church members. They increase the church's name recognition and establish a positive reputation in the community, even when done without any overt attempt to call attention to it. Kindness ministries involve random acts of kindness, opportunities to express God's love in a practical way.

I am aware of a church planting with a regular attendance of ten adults and a fifteen hundred dollar outreach budget that contacted twenty thousand people in just one year. Every contact involved at least a smile, a word of encouragement, and perhaps a handshake. In other words, these twenty thousand contacts involved real human interaction. How did the members of this very small church do it? They started with a table at the local community college's orientation day. They gave away writable computer disks (very popular), notebooks, pencils, cookies, brownies, cups for a soft drink, copies of outreach magazines, and entry forms for a prize drawing. Members sat at the table and offered a smile, answered questions, and assured students that everything was free. Contacts were made at the rate of fifty or so an hour, and many students took the outreach materials.

The same group supplied treats and stickers for children at the city's annual parade, roses to hospitals on Mother's Day, and Christmas ornaments and cookies to local fire and police departments. They gave out thousands of valentines declaring God's love. For Father's Day, they gave small tape measures to dads, along with the words to the popular song, "The Measure of a Man." Depending on the situation, the group has given away sunscreen, toilet paper, light bulbs, and rulers.

People who participate in kindness ministries usually want to do it again because of the sheer joy people get out of doing something nice for others. And it doesn't usually take long before people ask questions and start contacting the church, often with heartfelt thanks for these small acts of kindness. When such a church group takes out an ad in the paper or puts a flyer on a bulletin board, many who see the publicity are already favorably disposed toward the church. Combining kindness ministries with community surveys is an excellent way of knowing and becoming known. For a fuller discussion of kindness ministries, with lots of ideas, see Steve Sjogren's books, *Conspiracy of Kindness: A Refreshing Approach to Sharing the Love of Jesus With Others, Changing the World With Kindness*, and *Irresistible Evangelism: Natural Ways to Open Others to Jesus*.

## Patience

Patience is extremely important when working with secular people. To move from a totally secular environment into a traditional Adventist environment is not going to happen in two or three weeks. In my experience the process takes at least two years in most cases. This is long-term salt ministry, and it may be more appropriate for lay members of the church than for pastors, since pastors are often transferred from place to place. The people who develop a relationship with a secular person need to be around when he or she goes all the way with Christ.

I remember one couple that I baptized. I officiated at their wedding and then baptized them a year later. On the day of their baptism the members were shocked; they thought that both were already members of the church. They had been Ingathering, they came to all the work-bees, they went to all the prayer meetings—they were at everything. They were as active and involved in the church as anyone could be. But it was two years before they were comfortable in making a total commitment to Christ in the context of the Adventist Church. They insisted, "We want to know what we're getting into first. We plan to become Seventh-day Adventists, but we're going to become Seventh-day Adventists when we understand *all* of what that means."

Mass media advertising has led to a situation in which educated secular people have difficulty believing anything that is offered in the public square. They don't make major changes quickly or easily. They know that "propaganda" is not interested in truth, only in persuasion. For this reason, any group that has strong convictions about its beliefs will find secular people in their midst very challenging. If we wish to have any significant impact on secular people, particularly postmoderns, we will need to temper our convictions with an attitude of honesty and openness to discovery.

In an Internet world, any organization's "dirty laundry" is likely to be exhibited on a Web site for all to see. Hiding our institutional faults is no longer an option. But the situation is redeemable when a church is open about its shortcomings and exhibits a learning attitude. Secular people, rather than being turned off by the fact that the church isn't perfect, are usually excited when we are willing to openly acknowledge and discuss our imperfections. They say, "At least you guys don't think that you have all the answers."

I once had an evangelist in one of my classes. He was not happy. He said, "In order to convert people you have to be confident in what you believe. But the way you are teaching, everything seems just a little uncertain."

I realized at that moment how much I speak and teach with the secular audience in mind. Rather than assertions of certainty, secular people need to be led a step at a time and allowed the chance to question and reword things.

I responded to the evangelist, "In a previous generation, Adventists thought that in order to do effective evangelism they had to have absolute confidence in the rightness of every position. People would be swayed by the certitude of the one presenting the gospel. And that may still be true for a lot of people, including some secular people of the blue-collar variety. But that approach usually backfires with more educated secular types, and it certainly does not connect with postmoderns."

Secular people are attracted to those who are willing to admit that their understanding of truth is subject to limitation and distortion. The open-forum setting is actually much more persuasive for them than an assertive lecture. Through listening and dialoguing, we show respect for the viewpoint of others and encourage a similar respect in return. Such an approach will require patience. Instead of a "canned" approach, working with secular people requires constant tweaking and fine-tuning. There is no size that fits all. Don't expect rapid conversions to Christian faith from the secular mainstream.

Educated, white-collar, secular people are not usually looking for the "true church." What they are delighted to find, however, is a community that is fully devoted to an open, honest, and continuing search for truth. Those who know God's Word will know that we see through a glass darkly (see 1 Corinthians 13:12) and that our knowledge of truth will continue to grow until the end (see Proverbs 4:18).

## Conclusion

This "how-to" chapter has been necessarily sketchy and suggestive, outlining only basic principles. Many will want specific ideas on how to approach secular people effectively. Since the best book I have ever read on the subject, James Engel's *Contemporary Christian Communications,* is now out of print, I share some of the most helpful suggestions from that book in the next chapter.

# CHAPTER FOURTEEN

# The Nuts and Bolts of Outreach

In the book *Contemporary Christian Communications,* James F. Engel outlines a sliding scale he calls the Spiritual Decision Process. He sees each person fitting somewhere on a scale that runs from "Awareness of Supreme Being" at one end to a well-educated, fully committed, church-participating follower of Jesus at the other end. One of the goals of creative listening is to determine just where each person is on the scale. Outreach that is appropriate to a person at one point on the scale may not be appropriate to someone at another part of the scale. It is obviously inappropriate, for example, to press a person to repent of his sins when he hasn't ever heard the gospel!

One-on-one outreach is successful whenever it helps people move down the scale in the direction of a decision for Christ. The ultimate goal—full commitment to Christ and His church—is likely to take quite a bit of time, as we noted in the previous chapter. As you continue reading, please refer to the Engel Scale on page 174.

What causes people to make spiritual progress down the chart? Engel notes five things:

1. Spiritual progress can begin when a person becomes aware of a felt need (Engel calls it *need activation*). People don't change unless the change is seen to benefit them in some tangible way. When a person is aware of a specific need, he becomes open to information that will help him meet that need.

2. When people become aware of a need they begin a *search for information*. They are particularly open to appropriate, need-oriented outreach at this time.

3. If in the course of their search for information they see that some element of the gospel or a church-based program will make a positive difference in their lives, the result will usually be a *change of beliefs*.

4. The fact that the gospel has made a positive difference in their lives and beliefs will normally lead to a change of *attitudes*.

5. A change of attitude leads to a change in *behavior*. Secular people often have an aversion to receiving information or help from any type of faith-based organization, particularly a Christian one. When interaction with Christians and Christian ideas meets needs and has a positive impact on a person's life and beliefs, the aversion will drop, and that person will be open to changes in behavior. At this point a person is close to a *decision* which, when taken, leads to *spiritual growth*.

Both modern and postmodern secular people respond best when the process is slow and respectful of their integrity. Decisions for Christ usually involve a lifetime process and many influences. Such decisions don't normally take place without some prior understanding of the gospel and its relevance for life. Thus, a great deal of patience is necessary in working with secular people who don't have such a prior understanding.

Consider your own personal spiritual history. How long did it take you to reach the level of Christian maturity you have attained now? How many different people played minor or major roles at different points? How did you feel when well-meaning Christians offered unsolicited advice? How often did your spiritual growth plateau or even backtrack a bit? One of the best ways to understand what secular people go through in their encounter with the gospel is to remember our own pace of spiritual development.

Most secular postmoderns will be found somewhere around -7 on the Spiritual Decision Process scale. They will have some awareness about God but probably know relatively little about the gospel. So, the primary goal of witness to such a person is helping them build a basic knowledge of the gospel. Given the barriers that we all have against persuasion, this is a lengthy process beginning with relationship building followed by much attention to felt needs. Over time and after much experimentation, a secular postmodern may be ready to hear the basics of the gospel. A call for decision in the early stages of this process is inappropriate.

Secular modern people, on the other hand, are likely to be at Stage -6 and may even be at Stage -5 in terms of their knowledge of the Christian faith or church affairs. The issue for them is not so much information or even beliefs, it is a negative attitude toward the gospel or toward those who have presented the gospel to them in the past. This condition is at least equally difficult to deal with, even if the person is an attending member of a church. In such cases, the challenge may be more unlearning than learning.

I don't want to overplay the distinction between moderns and postmoderns in these matters, however. While a secular modern person is more likely than a postmodern to have some knowledge of Christian faith and the gospel, the postmodern may combine relative ignorance with a hostility to Christian faith that is "in the air" of the secular culture. While the modern person may have rejected the gospel on the basis of negative experience, the postmodern just "knows" that the gospel is not the answer to the problems of his or her life.

So, in practice, reaching out to people at the upper end of the Engel scale involves much unlearning and re-teaching of basics, regardless of whether they are moderns or postmoderns. A desire to witness to people in the mainstream must be combined with a sensitivity to the stories and experiences they will tell about the shortcomings of Christian belief and the church. For them, the very things you cherish the most may seem like false gods or a failed dream. We must expect to have our composure as well as our assumptions challenged.

One of the special challenges of secular outreach is the relative lack of literature or packaged approaches for people at these stages. And most Christians are personally unprepared to cope with people whose knowledge of the gospel or interest in it are minimal. I wrote the book *The Day That Changed the World* specifically to meet this need. It covers topics of burning interest in today's world, leading a secular person gradually toward a basic appreciation that the gospel may be worth investigating. It can be an effective aid to people who are not yet open to a direct gospel approach.

The best source of appropriate materials for modern and postmodern secular people is the LIFEdevelopment approach based in Great Britain. LIFEdevelopment is a long-term evangelistic strategy aimed at people with "no initial interest in organized religion." LIFEdevelopment envisions approaching secular people at various stages of spiritual interest or noninterest. The first phase involves developing friendships and focused small groups ("Get Connected"). The second phase involves a series of television programs with Dwight Nelson that focus on life issues such as stress and forgiveness and offers a gentle introduction to Christian faith ("Evidence"). The third phase ("Mind the Gap") uses additional videos to introduce the gospel in nonthreatening ways. LIFEdevelopment has also produced an outstanding outreach journal for postmoderns. It is called *LIFE.info*. These and other resources are available at the Web site www.adventistresource .org.uk or at www.lifedevelopment.info.

Later phases of the LIFEdevelopment program include training and discipling so secular people who have found Christ can, in turn, become leaders and witnesses in the church. They also include information on worship renewal so that churches will become more relevant to the postmodern generation. LIFEdevelopment's goal is to be not just a program but a cyclical process, a way of life and witness, leading people into a saving relationship with Jesus Christ.

As we have noted in discussing the contrast between fortress-style ministry and salt-style ministry, evangelistic success must no longer be evaluated only in terms of decisions. Many who reach out to modern and postmodern secular people will never see large numbers of decisions, because they are dealing with people who are at the upper levels of the chart. Outreach should be considered successful if people move down the chart, whether or not a decision for Christ has been made. And this will be the most difficult and time-consuming part of the journey. Once the basics of the gospel have been established and a positive attitude is in place, moving from -5 to -2 usually happens much more rapidly. These are the stages where reaping-type events can play a role, provided they are designed with mainstream sensibilities in mind. People with a positive attitude toward the gospel (-4) are the people who are nearing approachability for decision.

## The secular path toward decision

How will the process of moving people down the Engel scale work in practice? When we encounter a person at the upper end of the scale, we can use creative listening to help him or her become aware of felt needs (not necessarily a need for the gospel). Spiritual progress is not likely to happen until a person feels a need for change. Awareness of felt needs opens the way for an initial decision that life change will be beneficial in some tangible way. Once people become open to change in an area of their lives, they are open to information on how and why to make that change.

*Openness to change.* Most secular people have little sense of felt need, however, until confronted by some catastrophic event such as a financial reverse, a major illness in the immediate family, divorce, or the death of a loved one. Various stages in the life cycle are also times when people are open to change. The two stages of life that are most open to change are the "Pulling Up Roots" stage, between ages eighteen and twenty-five in most cases, and the "Midlife Crisis" phase, somewhere between ages thirty-five and fifty. Any "targeting" of specific age groups in the secular mainstream probably should focus on these two stages.

During the first of the two "open points" in a person's life (ages eighteen to twenty-five), young people are moving from relying on their parents' beliefs to establishing a self-chosen or self-constructed belief system. This phase is often characterized by an identity crisis, and this is heightened in the postmodern context. The midlife transition (ages thirty-five to fifty), on the other hand, is a time when people reassess the dreams and the values that they have internalized. At this point there is a final casting aside of inappropriate role models (including parents and teachers). They will either seek personal renewal at this point (including changes in religious beliefs and practices) or resign themselves to the realities of their live.

During the other phases of the life cycle, people are relatively closed to change unless faced with a personal or family crisis. From the midtwenties to the midthirties or so, people are busy trying to establish their youthful dreams (occupational and marital choices, putting down roots). To the extent that they succeed, contentment may preclude the examination of alternative dreams, and to the extent that they fail, the midlife crisis period of openness will ensue.

In middle adulthood (ages forty-five to sixty) people tend to reduce their ambitions for change and put more emphasis on living consistently within the code of values they clarified in midlife. They are interested in personal relationships and individual fulfillment but usually within the limits of the worldview and beliefs they adopted or confirmed during midlife crisis. During late adulthood (sixty and beyond) the focus moves to retirement, which sometimes leads to a new search for life renewal but more often leads to resignation.

The most open period of life for reaching secular people, therefore, would seem to be the teen years through the early twenties. If people have not been reached with the gospel by then, the best remaining opportunities will be during a midlife or late-life crisis. Crisis can come at any time and for any reason, but it is most often found around the age of forty and around the time of retirement. So, outreach programs aimed at secular people are most likely to be successful if targeted to young people, midlife adults, or transitioning senior citizens. But a felt-need-based relationship with a genuine Christian can create openness at any age. People in the "closed to change" stages of life, however, will require more time and skill on the part of the Christian trying to reach them.

*Gaining knowledge.* When people discover unmet needs in their lives, they begin a search for information that will help them to meet those needs. The search process will cover as many sources as are available to the individual, including television, the Internet, books, magazines, the advice of friends, and, if the need is pressing, even strangers. The greatest opportunity to reach secular postmoderns comes in providing needed information at the right time. An appropriate use of magazine ads, radio spots, and creative self-help books, therefore, can arouse interest in people whose search for information has been activated by a felt need.

Distributing tracts, on the other hand, is largely a waste of time and money unless the tracts are specifically aimed at a felt need of the person receiving the tract. Even then, a tract is most likely to be read when it is received from a trusted personal friend rather than from a stranger on the street or in a passing car.

Christian television can play a role in providing information for those in the search process. By itself, it can also move people a step or two down the Engel scale. But churches should not operate under the illusion that TV broadcasting or podcasting alone can carry people along the entire journey. For full evangelistic effect, television programming must be combined with personal contact in various forms.

Home or public meetings can also play an important role at this stage of a person's developing interest. People will go out of their way to attend meetings that are specifically focused on areas of felt need unless they get the impression that those holding the meeting have an agenda. It is imperative, therefore, that those who do public meetings in the mainstream environment be very attentive to integrity and authenticity. We must be genuinely willing to make a difference in people's lives whether or not they end up agreeing with us or joining our group. And we need to be willing to speak the language of those we are seeking to help.

*Changing beliefs and attitudes.* At the point of information search it becomes possible for a person's attitudes and beliefs to progress toward a decision for Christ. When an idea has made a positive difference in a person's life, it is much more likely to become part of his ongoing belief system. If the idea is associated with a Christian or a Christian group, that person's attitude toward Christian faith is likely to become more positive. But in most cases moderns and postmodern secular people change in small increments rather than in leaps and bounds.

It is at this stage that a sensitive two-horizon Christian comes in handy. The probability that a person will make even small changes in his or her beliefs is directly proportional to the credibility of the one inviting change. And the credibility of a Christian's witness is determined less by words than by the character of the person's life. If we have earned credibility with a secular person, he will consult with us when he is considering changes in beliefs and attitudes.

*Encouraging a decision.* Although psychology is helpful at many points in the decision process, conversion is a divine work. The Christian's part in a secular person's decision process is gentle, friendly encouragement. Persuasion is up to God alone. "And the Lord's servant must not quarrel; instead, he must be kind to everyone, able to teach, not resentful. Those who oppose him he must gently instruct, in the hope that God will grant them repentance leading them to a knowledge of the truth, and that they will come to their senses and escape from the trap of the devil, who has taken them captive to do his will" (2 Timothy 2:24–26, NIV).

When it comes to decision time, the Bible encourages us not to be argumentative but rather to be gentle and teachable, remembering how long and hard our own journey to faith has been. In a real sense, people who believe and practice destructive things have rarely made a conscious decision to pursue such a course. They have fallen into Satan's trap. We have no capacity in ourselves to release them from the trap, no matter how aggressively we try. A forceful approach at this time may even drown out the still, small Voice of the Spirit. But through loving humility we can help create an atmosphere in which the Holy Spirit can move a secular person to decision.

## Activating a sense of need

The entire process of movement toward decision is grounded on the basic awareness of felt need. People generally will not change unless they feel the need to change. But Engel goes on to note that in the Western mainstream many people feel or express no awareness of need. Thus, the first step in helping people progress in the spiritual decision process may involve the activation of need. Anyone can be reached, provided they are reached at the level of one of their felt needs. But what do you do when someone doesn't seem to feel any need?

The best known analysis of human need was developed by Abraham Maslow. Maslow developed a hierarchy of five human needs. He described these five needs as (1) physical, (2) safety, (3) belonging and love, (4) esteem, and (5) self-actualization. While all five needs are important, one does not become aware of the higher needs (nos. 4 and 5) as long as the lower ones are unfulfilled.

The basic level of needs involves survival, physical necessities, and safety. The fundamental human need is a physical one. People need food, drink, clothing, and a reasonable degree of shelter in order to survive. The apostle Paul recognized the importance of these needs (see 1 Timothy 6:7, 8). Contentment is a possibility wherever the need for food, clothing, and shelter is being met.

The second fundamental need is the need for safety. When people have enough to eat and a minimal amount of clothing and shelter, they become concerned about protecting what they have. In a community where crime or environmental issues threaten physical safety, people feel insecure regarding their physical needs even when those needs are being met for the time being.

Although much of the Western world has attained an unprecedented level of human comfort, the majority of people in the world still live in places where life is dominated by physical hardships. In such situations people are often profoundly unhappy; life is a bleak and frustrating experience. Where such conditions exist, the first obligation of the church is to do all it can to remedy these underlying conditions (see Luke 4:18, 19). In these places, feeding and sheltering people becomes the gospel of God's grace and mercy to those who need Him. But when oppression or demographic necessity make it impossible to fully provide for basic human needs, the remaining option is to emphasize the rewards of the next life. Where physical safety is an issue that the church can do nothing about, the gospel can still offer freedom from anxiety as people shelter their minds and hearts in God's purpose for them.

When physical and safety needs have been met, people are freed to focus on the need to give and receive love, the need for a sense of community. During the Depression, everyone was worried about food and shelter. As America came out of the Depression, people focused more on security. They saved and worked to ensure that they would never have to go through something like that again. In the process the need for love and community sometimes received little attention. As a result, the postmodern generation, for whom physical survival is largely assumed in the Western world, has focused on love and community with a vengeance, blaming their "boomer" parents for concentrating on basic needs at the expense of love and community.

The church has the opportunity to meet this need for belonging through a true sense of community. Whenever we do evangelism we need to also ask the question as to what kind of community we will be bringing people to. Secular people will not stay for long in a community that is phony or divided over what seem to them to be nonessential issues.

Postmoderns, in particular, will test the quality of community before they are willing to consider the ideas that hold that community together. Belonging comes before believing in their case. And community does not come from the worship service alone. People need to belong for more than just an hour or two a week. Small groups, outreach projects, social events, and more are needed for a community to feel like more than just another thing on the to-do list.

The fourth level of need has to do with self-worth, the sense that you are precious, unique, and capable. This need is also activated after the basic survival needs are cared for. Self-worth or self-esteem is a major point of concern in the secular world today. The gospel addresses this need powerfully, as I demonstrate in the tenth chapter of my book *Meet God Again for the First Time*. Secular people seek for value in possessions, performance, and in relationship with others. But none of these three satisfies for very long. Our need for self-worth can be truly met only in relationship with Jesus Christ.

Maslow's description of the highest level of need comes very close to a need for the gospel; he calls it the need for self-actualization. For Maslow, the need for self-actualization is met through creative activity at the highest level. But if this were truly the ultimate attainment, actors, professional musicians, artists, and novelists would be the most fulfilled people on earth. But this is clearly not a given.

The gospel teaches us that self-actualization is ultimately possible only in a life surrendered to God's purpose. When we realize the value we have in the eyes of God and when we give our lives over to the purpose for which He has designed us, we attain the highest level of meaning and fulfillment. To some degree this need cannot be met by mere success or creativity. It is met by the cumulative sense that life is being lived according to God's design and purpose. Rick Warren's book *The Purpose-Driven Life* has been helpful to many in response to this need, although there are elements of the book that are challenging from an Adventist perspective.

The awareness of need is often precipitated by a catastrophic event in a person's life. Events like divorce, death of a spouse, or incarceration can seriously jar a person's confidence in his place in life. They can lead to a crumbling of the defense mechanisms that mask a person's awareness of need. In those situations people are more open to a sensitive presentation of the gospel than at any other. While other events, such as a job change, graduation, or buying a house are also surprisingly stressful, they do not have the weight of the above. But an accumulation of minor stressors also can work together to precipitate a strong sense of crisis in a person's life. People are especially open to information and relationship when stress levels are high.

Engel, therefore, includes a social readjustment scale, which can help anyone assess the level of stress he or she is under at a given moment. The higher the cumulative number related to stressful events in one's life, the greater the level of stress. The greater the stress in one's life, the greater the awareness of felt needs. People under a great deal of stress will be more open to the right kind of approach with the gospel. On the other hand, great gospel patience is needed with those who feel little or no need.

I conclude this chapter with the social readjustment scale and the Engel Spiritual Decision Process scale. Cumulative numbers of 300 or higher on the social readjustment scale indicate a significant amount of stress.

## The Effect of Change on Social Readjustment

| Life Event | Mean Value |
| --- | --- |
| 1. Death of a spouse | 100 |
| 2. Divorce | 73 |
| 3. Marital separation from mate | 65 |
| 4. Detention in jail or other institution | 63 |
| 5. Death of a close family member | 63 |
| 6. Major personal injury or illness | 53 |
| 7. Marriage | 50 |
| 8. Being fired at work | 47 |
| 9. Marital reconciliation with mate | 45 |
| 10. Retirement from work | 45 |
| 11. Major change in the behavior of a family member | 44 |
| 12. Pregnancy | 40 |

13. Sexual difficulties                                          39

14. Gaining a new family member (e.g., through
    birth, adoption, oldster moving in, marriage, etc.) 39

15. Major business readjustment (e.g., merger,
    reorganization, bankruptcy, etc.)

16. Major change in financial state (e.g., a lot worse
    off or a lot better off than usual)                      38

17. Death of a close friend                                   37

18. Changing to a different line of work                    36

19. Major change in the number of arguments with
    spouse  (e.g., either a lot more or a lot less than
    usual regarding child rearing, personal habits, etc.) 35

20. Taking on a mortgage greater than $10,000
    (e.g., purchasing a home, business, etc.)             31

21. Foreclosure on a mortgage or loan                    30

22. Major change in responsibilities at work
    (e.g., promotion, demotion, lateral transfer)         29

23. Son or daughter leaving home (e.g., marriage,
    college)                                                      29

24. In-law troubles                                              29

25. Outstanding personal achievement                     28

26. Wife beginning or ceasing work outside the home  26

27. Beginning or ceasing formal schooling               26

28. Major change in living conditions (e.g., building
    a new home, remodeling, deterioration of home
    or neighborhood)                                          25

29. Revision of personal habits (dress, manners, etc.) 24

30. Troubles with the boss 23

31. Major change in working hours or conditions 20

32. Change in residence 20

33. Changing to a new school 20

34. Major change in usual type and/or amount of
    recreation 19

35. Major change in church activities (e.g., a lot
    more or less than usual) 19

36. Major change in social activities (e.g., clubs,
    movies, dances) 18

37. Taking on a mortgage or loan less than $10,000
    (car, TV) 17

38. Major change in sleeping habits
    (e.g., a lot more or less than usual, or change in
    part of the day when asleep) 16

39. Major change in number of family get-togethers
    (more or less) 15

40. Major change in eating habits (more or less,
    or different) 15

41. Vacation 13

42. Christmas 12

43. Minor violations of the law (e.g., traffic tickets,
    jaywalking, disturbing the peace, etc.) 11

**The Spiritual Decision Process**
**(showing the stages of spiritual growth)**

| God's Role | Communicator's Role | | Man's Response |
|---|---|---|---|
| General Revelation | | -8 | Awareness of Supreme Being |
| Conviction ↓ | Proclamation ↓ | -7 | Some knowledge of gospel |
| | | -6 | Knowledge of fundamentals of gospel |
| | | -5 | Grasp of personal implications of gospel |
| | | -4 | Positive attitude toward act of becoming a Christian |
| | | -3 | Problem recognition and intention to act |
| | Call for Decision ↓ | -2 | Decision to act |
| | | -1 | Repentance and faith in Christ |
| REGENERATION | | | NEW CREATURE |
| Sanctification ↓ | Follow up ↓ | +1 | Postdecision evaluation |
| | | +2 | Incorporation into church |
| | Cultivation ↓ | +3 | Conceptual and behavioral growth<br>• Communion with God<br>• Stewardship<br>• Internal reproduction<br>• External reproduction |
| | | | Eternity |

# CHAPTER FIFTEEN

# Mending the Disconnect Between Church and Society

Life might be simpler if reaching out to modern and postmodern secular people were purely a one-on-one activity. But one cannot reach out to the secular mainstream in a vacuum. At some point one needs to confront the inevitable tension between the way the church does things and the way mainstream people respond. We have to struggle with the question of how the Adventist horizon and the secular horizon can come together without compromising the best qualities of either. So, at some point we have to ask the question of what a local church or conference can do to make a bigger impact in the secular environment.

## Educate the church

First of all, churches and groups of Adventists need to be educated regarding the challenges of both secularism and postmodernism. Many still believe that the strategies of the past will work if implemented with sufficient faith and vigor. But while faith, prayer, and a principled commitment to Adventist beliefs and standards need not present barriers to secular people, church business as usual will not accomplish the task. Secular postmoderns, in particular, need and deserve a whole new way of outreach, as we have seen.

We also need to educate the church about the problem of horizons. Members need to know that without a lot of listening and learning we will not be effective in reaching secular neighbors, friends, and family. In the process it is helpful to point out that the Bible does not offer a single, rigid model for outreach and evangelism. Since most human beings are uncomfortable with change, it helps to learn that change in the area of outreach will bring us into conformity with Scripture rather than the reverse.

## Multiply ministries

As part of the process of education, we need to encourage a multiplicity of ministries. Secular people are diverse. They tend to respond in unique ways and are not normally reached in large groups. The only way, therefore, to counter the pluralism of society is with the pluralism of the Holy Spirit, an explosion of all kinds of outreach ministries empowered by the Spirit (see John 3:8). This will not come from central planning but from the members discovering the unique roles God has purposed for everyone.

Nothing will energize the laity as much as discovering God's unique plan for each person's life and outreach. No pastor can reach the secular community by himself or herself. It takes an army of people working under the empowerment of the Spirit. When a church activates the energy of the Spirit, it is amazing the different kinds of ministries that will emerge. A spirit-driven multiplicity of ministries is the perfect compliment to the incredible diversity of secular postmodernism.

## The role of the workplace

One of the best places to implement secular outreach is the workplace. It is in the workplace, not at church, that Seventh-day Adventists come in contact with the mainstream of society. But many opportunities are lost because the outreach possibilities of the workplace are either misused or go unnoticed. We must not allow misguided or unethical attempts to evangelize the workplace to steer us away from our best opportunity. The workplace provides opportunities for relationship with secular postmoderns. It also provides the context for demonstrating the difference that Christian faith can make in the nonreligious environment.

If the workplace is the best place for evangelism, then Seventh-day Adventists are needed everywhere in the workplace. The possibilities for making a difference in the mainstream culture are especially large in media, education, journalism, and the arts. These are the occupations that have the greatest influence over people. Adventists involved in media or the arts will face serious challenges, including much criticism from fellow believers. But they will be acting in harmony with counsel we received many years ago: "Men are needed who pray to God for wisdom, and who, under the guidance of God, can put new life into the old methods of labor and can invent new plans and new methods of awakening the interest of church members and reaching the men and women of the world" (*Evangelism,* p. 105).

"Means will be devised to reach hearts. Some of the methods used in this work will be different from the methods used in the work in the past; but let no one, because of this, block the way by criticism" (*Review and Herald,* September 30, 1902).

## Encourage constructive change in worship

Although public evangelism often succeeds in increasing baptisms, it does not always result in sustained church growth. One reason is that the people didn't join a Saturday morning church. They joined a church that met five nights a week, used lots of visual aids, and had exciting music performed by professionals. After baptism, people are expected to settle for once a week, few visual aids if any, and a piano or organ played with a minimum of enthusiasm. A little reflection indicates that the quality of Sabbath worship is crucial to sustaining church growth—and not just among secular people.

Many Adventist churches are finding that a relevant and vibrant worship service has powerful, word-of-mouth drawing power upon the unchurched. Those who have fallen away from church attendance because the worship service seemed boring, manipulative, and out of touch with their lives are often open to giving church another chance when the worship service is interesting and speaks powerfully to real issues in the real world.

Part of this worship renewal includes a use of contemporary language and harmonic idioms. While this has appeared threatening to some, history teaches us that revivals of faith are usually accompanied by revivals of Christian songwriting. The need for fresh melodies, styles, and lyrics lies in the fact that faith must touch base with real life if it is to become the everyday experience that is needed to overcome secular drift. Contemporary secular songs, though often presenting messages that are contrary to the gospel, nevertheless express deeply the struggles of life in today's world. When Christian music demonstrates an awareness of those contemporary struggles, it has a powerful influence in behalf of the gospel's solutions to those struggles.

None of us are fully insulated from contemporary life. Though we may shun the television and radio, we are influenced nevertheless. When you call a bank, a store, or the credit-card company, they put you on hold and put pop music on the phone. When you go to the grocery store or the shopping mall to obtain items necessary for life, similar kinds of music are playing in the background. It is impossible to live totally in a world other than our own. So, when worship fails to speak to the world we live in, it is easy to live a double life. One is the life that we live when we are in church or associate with fellow Christians. The other is the life we live as we work and play. Such a compartmentalized life will neither save us from secular drift nor attract secular people to our faith.

Change, however, can be a very wrenching experience for church people, even when the positive results are dramatic. Many people do appreciate a more traditional worship style. Many of the great hymns of the church still speak powerfully. Radical changes in this area may do more harm than good in a traditional church. But there are a number of simple things that could enhance any church service to meet the needs of more traditional Adventists, on the one hand, while still providing a more user-friendly environment for secular people.

*1. Everyday language.* A noncontroversial, yet significant, enhancement to worship is the use of common, everyday language in prayer, praise, and preaching. While it may take a while for people to learn how to do this, the goal is to express all aspects of our faith in the kind of language that is understood on the street, rather than in the specialized language of Adventism. It is incredibly frustrating to be involved in a search for God only to discover that you will have to learn a new language in order to learn anything about Him from His people! God meets people where they are, so when we are using everyday language, we are following His example.

But more than this, the use of common language expresses caring. When we meet people where they are, it communicates that we care enough to understand where they are coming from. They matter to us. When people know that they matter to other humans, it is easier for them to believe that they matter also to God. The use of everyday language makes God real to people whose lives are lived in a world that is quite different from the insulated world of the church.

*2. Take-home value.* A second enhancement to worship in the secular postmodern context is to make sure that whatever happens on Sabbath morning has high "take-home value;" in other words, that it is of practical use outside of Sabbath hours. People need to hear things they can apply on Monday, Tuesday, and Wednesday mornings. A demonstration of practical, living Christianity is an attractive force that invites others to inquire further into godliness. Yet Adventist worship often contains little that would change the world on any other day of the week. Perhaps the following painful indictment is relevant: "It is a sad fact that the reason why many dwell so much on theory and so little on practical godliness is that Christ is not abiding in their hearts. They do not have a living connection with God" (*Testimonies for the Church,* vol. 4, pp. 395, 396).

We will become effective in presenting how a Christian copes with Monday morning when we ourselves have wrestled honestly with the issues people face at home, in the neighborhood, and on the job. When we ourselves know how to walk with God every day of the week, we will be able to teach others to do the same. The churches that are making the greatest impact on mainstream society today are emphasizing practical Christianity. In saying this, I do not mean a devaluation of doctrine. But the teaching of doctrine needs to be life-changing, not just mind-changing.

*3. Excellence.* A third area that makes a big difference with secular people is a concern for excellence, for quality, in everything we do as a church. Too often, Adventist churches look shabby and outdated. The sermon and special music seem thrown together at the last minute. Adventists may tolerate shabbiness, but secular people consider shabbiness to be an insult both to their intelligence and to their stewardship of time.

Although we demand quality in the products we buy, the motels we stay in, or the programming we enjoy, we somehow expect an unchurched person to enjoy a halfhearted sermon and a thoroughly butchered song. Less than the best isn't good enough anymore. The music, the scripture reading, prayer, and even the announcements are worthy of careful planning and skilled execution.

One of the best ways to enhance excellence in any operation is to frequent critical evaluations. As threatening as evaluation may be, if we are serious about excellence, we need to constantly get feedback regarding the quality of our efforts for God. The ministries and services of a church should frequently be measured in relation to the Word of God and the needs of the people being served. No one should consider themselves exempt, not even the pastor. The evaluation process is always painful but results in more effective ministry.

4. *Grab people's attention.* A fourth area that can make a difference is directly related to the reality of the media. Worship needs to be more visual and attention-grabbing than ever before. In a media age people's attention cannot be taken for granted. Postmoderns, in particular, are spending less and less time with books and more and more time with visual media. Many see more words in digital format—Internet, TV, e-mail, computer-generated documents, etc.—than in printed form. Postmoderns prefer a picture to a thousand words. If you argue a case in propositions, they probably will not remember what you said. But if you share a powerful metaphor or paint a picture with words, they are much more likely to understand and remember.

Postmoderns have grown up with so many options that they are easily bored. Have you ever watched a young person with a remote control and 150 channels to choose from? In today's world, people decide in five or ten seconds whether the sermon is worth taking seriously. But rightly handled, a judicious use of visual media can provide an environment in which modern and postmodern people can connect with a message. The church needs to become three-dimensional, using images, not as a substitute for words, but in support of words.

Music, if it is done well, can enhance the attention quotient of a worship service. The visual arts can bring home spiritual lessons with incredible power. If the people in your church are dead set against the word *drama,* utilize a children's story instead. Coordinate it with the sermon, the hymns, and the scripture reading; make the whole service one of a piece. Adults love the children's story—often more than the children do! It *is* possible to make the worship service more interesting without offending everybody.

In the modern era, worship was focused on *learning* about God. In the postmodern era worship needs to be much more about *experiencing* God. And there is a strong biblical basis for this. In the Old Testament sanctuary, all the senses were engaged; worship was more than just listening to a preacher. There was visual drama, there was the smell of incense, the taste of food offerings, the action of the participants. At some of the feasts people participated with percussion instruments and sacred dancing (see Psalm 150). Men and women were separated during the dancing, of course. Temple worship was a multisensory experience. To grab people's attention is also in harmony with the example of Christ who had a fascinating way of asking little rhetorical questions such as, "Which of these two sons really obeyed his father?"

5. *Strong, spiritual tone.* A strong, spiritual tone is critical to worship renewal. Truth is not enough to keep people in church today. People need to experience a living God. When secular postmodern people decide to come to church, it is because they sense that the living God is present there. They are drawn to churches where the people know God and know how to teach others to know Him. Everything that is done, whether it is the sermon, the special music, or the prayer, needs to be driven by the spiritual vitality of those who participate. Secular people are not easily fooled. If the spiritual life of the church is phony, it will fool no one—certainly not the church's own youth.

6. *Authenticity.* This brings us to the sixth area of potential improvement in Adventist worship, and probably the most important one. People today are crying out for examples of genuine, authentic Christianity—or to use street terms, "being real." So often in Adventist churches, people are just going through the motions, playing church. But secular postmodern people seem to have a sixth sense about who is genuine and who is not. They can smell phony Christians a mile away.

Authenticity builds on spirituality. The most effective path to true authenticity is to cultivate genuineness each day in a devotional encounter with God. Christ can help you to see yourself as others see you. In Christ it is possible to learn how to truly be yourself. As we reach out to the secular people in our communities, we will discover that one of the best ways to find the point of contact in another person is through our own confession of need. People are reluctant to make themselves vulnerable to others. But if we allow ourselves to be vulnerable with them (at the appropriate time and in an appropriate way), they may feel comfortable to share their deepest needs and concerns with us. I have written at length on this important subject in my book *Knowing God in the Real World.*

Because of their skepticism toward authority and the institutions of authority, postmodern people will explore the claims of Christianity only through individual Christians who have gained their respect and trust. They will not believe what a Christian says; they will look to see how he or she lives. They will be more impressed if that person is self-consciously fallible than if he or she hides the defects of their lives at home. The main question about religion in postmodern minds is not "Is it true?" but "Is it real?" The church does not need to be perfect, but it had better be authentic.

## An example of contemporary worship

I am privileged to have been able to watch the development of powerful, life-changing contemporary worship at Pioneer Memorial Church (Andrews University) over the last twenty years. To my knowledge, this has become the best example of the above principles in the Adventist Church. Under the guidance of Dwight Nelson and his pastoral staff, college-age youth have sought that fine balance between a slavish adherence to the ways of the past and complete acceptance of all contemporary idioms. Over twenty years, several generations of students have tweaked and tweaked the process.

The result is a thrilling blend of organ, piano, guitars, and, at times, violins, trumpets, and the light use of percussion. Grand hymns are introduced in fresh ways. New songs are prayed over and explained to more traditional members. The worship leaders exercise care and thoughtfulness in the way they dress and comport themselves on the platform. There have been times when the worship has ministered God to me in ways I have experienced nowhere else. Worship has occurred with an intensity I had not imagined human beings were capable of. And the icing on the cake has been the directness, energy, depth, humor, and spiritual passion with which God has graced Dwight Nelson. As I write, you can experience "Pioneer worship" every week at www.pmchurch.tv. And the church is filled every Sabbath with youth and young adults. The postmodern generation is plugged in and turned on to God every week.

But let me caution you. The power of worship at Pioneer Memorial Church did not happen overnight. Dwight Nelson has committed himself to stay with the process for more than twenty years. There have been fits and starts. There has been criticism and tears. Some have complained that things didn't go far enough. Others have complained that things went too far. The process has been tweaked many times. But a combination of talent, perseverance, prayer, and long-term commitment (on the part of the pastoral staff and congregation) has resulted in a life-changing experience from week to week. My own children, who range from teenagers to young adults, have all been strongly confirmed in their Adventist faith by the ministry of this church.

So, be prepared to exercise patience where worship is concerned. It will take time to get things right. And "right" will be a little different in different places and cultures. I have experienced powerful worship that is attractive to postmoderns in places like Fiji, Australia, eastern and southern Africa, Germany, and Norway, as well as North America. There is no set formula for every place. Each church needs to bring its passion for the lost to the foot of the Cross and be open to God's leading for that situation. The church exists for mission; mission does not exist for the church.

## Transitioning secular people into the church

No matter how "seeker friendly" a worship service may be, there is much about the corporate personality of traditional churches that makes it hard for secular people, whether modern or postmodern, to feel at home there. This is particularly true while they are in the search process. So, a critical component of any outreach to mainstream society must be the provision of some sort of "halfway house" between the world and the church. Other ways to express this idea are "subcultures" and a "door" into the church just for secular people. These subcultures can occur in small groups, distinctive worship services, or nontraditional gatherings (such as parties or focused seminars) in a neutral location.

The idea of a "halfway house" arose in the context of the attempt to transition the mentally ill from confinement in a traditional "asylum" to full function within society. It was recognized that the huge gap between the two social locations would be difficult to bridge without a lot of help. The "halfway house" provided enough elements of the asylum situation to assure routine and a certain comfort zone while the patients learned the skills they would need to adapt to mainstream society. I have adopted the metaphor to illustrate the importance of providing a comfort zone for secular people as they manage the difficult transition from the secular mainstream to becoming fully devoted members of the house of faith. The term *subculture* illustrates that this halfway house will have elements of church but in a context that does not automatically turn off the secular seeker.

The spiritual halfway house, therefore, is a setting where secular people who are interested in faith but who don't yet fit into the church socially or politically can get the spiritual direction they need. Although "church" is usually designed with the needs and interests of traditional members in mind, the goal of the "subculture" is to operate in such a way that the needs and interests of the target audience drive everything that is done. A subculture aimed at the secular mind-set would intentionally avoid the minor irritations that drive secular people away from churches.

By means of these subcultures, one can provide a door to the church for people who wouldn't feel at home in the church otherwise. Over a period of time, many secular people will gradually make the transition from the subculture into the main body of the church. Others may attend the sub-culture for two or three years and indicate no further interest in the church. Patience will certainly need to be the watchword in a true "halfway house." It takes time for people out of the mainstream to be integrated into Ad-ventist ways of thinking and doing. But when we realize how long God has waited for us to come around on one issue or another, we will want to deal with people the way He has dealt with us.

Ultimately, this patience is grounded in the love God gives us for those who don't know Him. We are patient with secular people because they are souls "for whom Christ died" (Romans 14:15, KJV). God energizes us with His love and gives us the skills and attitudes we need to connect with those who don't know Him (see 1 Corinthians 12:8–11). We meet people where they are because that is what God does. The result is a community of faith where people of diverse backgrounds and experiences learn how to please God and make a difference in this world.

It's a new kind of friendship.

# CHAPTER SIXTEEN

# Stages of Friendship

One of the most challenging things about reaching out to modern and postmodern secular people is the time and effort it takes to reach people one by one. Public meetings have their place, but in working with the secular mainstream there is no substitute for serious involvement in the personal lives of others. To do so effectively, however, requires a keen sense of where relationships are and the stages through which they pass. It would be helpful, therefore, to review the stages of friendship and explore their implications for personal outreach to people in the secular mainstream.

Many writers have addressed this issue in different ways. I find the seven-step approach developed by two friends, Bill Underwood and Ed Dickerson, to be the most helpful.* If you keep these stages in mind, you can tell exactly where you are in each of your relationships with secular people. You also know exactly what must happen for the relationship to progress to the next stage.

At each stage of relationship both parties need to be willing to progress for the relationship to develop further. If one party holds back, the relationship will stall at the level both parties are willing to work with. If you

---

* Based on personal discussions with Dr. Bill Underwood, the original source of the seven-stages scheme, and Ed Dickerson, who has developed them further and brought them to my attention. I have tweaked the system from my own experience, so please do not hold these two gentlemen responsible for any shortcomings I may have introduced here.

try to move one or two stages ahead of the other person (as often happens in canned witnessing exchanges), the relationship is likely to terminate unless the aggressive party backs off.

## 1. Acquaintance

When they first meet, people exchange greetings and comments about the weather or whatever else they immediately know they have in common. They may take quick stock of the other person's face, body type, and surface personality, weighing whether they want to enter into a deeper relationship or leave things on the surface. At this stage, the other person is a "nodding acquaintance." There is little or no risk at this stage.

We encounter many people in this category nearly every day. In most cases, we don't even know the other person's name. Most acquaintances never get much closer to us than a greeting. Circumstances may precipitate a deeper relationship, but movement to the next stage usually means that one of the parties, at least, is interested in going a little deeper. When it comes to witnessing, of course, the one wanting to move the relationship to a deeper level is the one who would like to share his or her faith with the other.

## 2. Facts and reports

The second stage of friendship involves the exchange of facts and reports. At this stage you reveal things that are of interest to you, that have some importance in your life. To put it another way, you reveal things that are personal but not private. At this stage the risk in the relationship is small, but there is some risk. You are testing the water of relationship with ideas that are central to who you are. If the other person proves uninterested in the things you reveal, some pain can be involved.

When it comes to witnessing, or one-on-one outreach, this is where the point of contact first comes in. A relationship can grow if the two individuals have common interests. Felt needs are a strong point of interest in a person's life. If you share an interest in those things and you have something constructive to say about them, the relationship will move past stage one into the second stage—exchange of useful information.

## 3. Opinions and judgments

When individuals move to the third stage, the level of risk is considerably greater. When you know someone a little better, you have a sense of what he can handle and what he can't. If you want to go deeper with another person, you must be willing to share some of your opinions and judgments. You don't talk just about the weather. You throw out an opinion about politics or the latest world events, checking to see if the other person is safe to go deeper with. If you find the other person to be a "kindred spirit" on a lot of issues, the relationship is likely to progress even further.

This is the stage where issues of faith come in, since the secular person considers faith issues to be opinions and judgments rather than facts. To be rejected for one's opinions is more painful than to be rejected for an inappropriate greeting or a misstated fact. Our opinions and judgments lie closer to the core of our being. It is vital in witnessing, therefore, not to jeopardize a relationship on the basis of opinions that are not vital to the process of building faith. It is easy to scuttle outreach relationships because of peripheral ideas, things that are not vital to a biblical worldview.

## 4. Feelings

Friends reach Stage 4 when they are willing to share feelings as well as facts or opinions. Human beings are very vulnerable at the stage of feelings. If you share how you feel, and the other person rejects that feeling, it can be quite devastating. So, people will often move into this stage very gingerly. As the relationship deepens, people become willing to share what makes them happy and sad. They are willing to share what makes them angry or afraid. To share one's emotions is to become vulnerable to another. When that vulnerability is respected and affirmed by both parties, the relationship can go deeper yet.

In many cultures it's common for people to express feelings of anger, but other feelings, such as fear, happiness, or sadness, may be suppressed. When someone is willing to share his true feelings with you, he is trusting you a great deal. The Bible is full of emotional language, language of the heart and soul. If we want to truly affect the inner lives of others, we must not be afraid to be open about our own feelings.

## 5. Failures and mistakes

Stage 5 is the make or break point in many relationships. In Stage 5 people become willing to share, not only their opinions and judgments, their joys and fears, but they are willing to open up about their failures and mistakes. It takes a high level of trust in another person before most of us are willing to say "I was wrong." To avoid going to this level of relationship, we make excuses or accusations when we are confronted. If a person becomes defensive when you ask leading questions, it probably is time to back off to the previous level of relationship and give him time to learn that he can trust you at the next level. In Stage 5 we become truly vulnerable with each other.

## 6. Accountability

At this stage, the level of trust has become so high that we are willing to allow the other person to point out our faults. One could call this the stage of accountability. We are willing to allow the other person to hold us accountable in our personal life. We give him permission to confront us whenever our behavior is damaging to ourselves, to others, or to our relationship with him. We allow another person some control over our lives.

One of the problems in marriage is that we often confront one another as if we were at Stage 6, but the other partner's defensiveness makes it clear that we have not been given permission to operate at this level. A similar problem arises in one-on-one outreach. We feel a need to confront others about their behaviors or beliefs, but if we have not welcomed similar intimacy from them, the relationship has become one-sided, and our approach is likely to be rejected. When the other party is defensive, we need to back off to an earlier stage and pray for the Holy Spirit's softening influence on our own hearts as well as on the other person.

## 7. Total Intimacy

Stage 7 is the stage of total intimacy, the place where we keep no secrets from each other. At this stage everything is open and transparent to the other person. This stage is something that is rarely achieved on this earth, although it is a worthy goal for deep friendships and for marriages.

## Conclusion

After sharing these seven stages with a group, Ed likes to ask the question, "If we apply these seven stages of friendship to our relationship with God, at what stage does conversion occur?" Ed believes that conversion occurs when we are at Stage 5 with God, the stage where we are willing to share our faults with Him, what we usually call confession of sin. So, the process of creative listening is designed to take us through the stages of friendship with a secular person until we reach the stage where that other person is vulnerable enough to receive the gospel. Awareness of these stages will help us to track how the relationship is going, to avoid going too fast or too slow. It helps to minimize the serious bumps that tend to happen along the way to spiritual friendship.

But there is something in this that troubles me. When I ask people where in the stages of friendship most Adventist churches are, people normally answer "Stage 3." In other words, relationships in the typical Adventist church center on opinions and judgments. Most Adventists do not move on easily to feelings (Stage 4) or to a willingness to admit faults (Stage 5). Yet, these same church members believe—or hope—that they are in a saving relationship with God (Stage 5).

To put it starkly, there is an unwritten sense that the typical Adventist has a closer relationship with God than he or she does with other members of the church. We assume a Stage 5 relationship with God (confession of sin), yet are satisfied with a Stage 3 relationship with fellow believers.

Scripture warns us that this is an untenable situation. According to 1 John 4:20, "If anyone says, 'I love God,' yet hates his brother, he is a liar. For anyone who does not love his brother, whom he has seen, cannot love God, whom he has not seen" (NIV). In other words, John tells us that it is not possible to have a closer relationship with the Unseen than one has with living, breathing friends in the tangible world. If we find it difficult to go deep in relationship with others, we should not assume that we somehow have a much deeper relationship with the unseen God.

This suggests to me that we all can use a certain amount of relational therapy. To learn how to love and be loved is essential, not only to our well-being as social creatures but to our ability to go deep with God. And to the degree that we can go deep with both God and others, we will be effective in helping others attain a similar relationship with Him.

## Final words

Perhaps the bottom line of this book is this: We cannot share what we don't have. We cannot bring secular people to God if we don't know Him ourselves. We cannot bring secular people to God unless we are willing to share ourselves in deep relationship with them. Our capacity for changing the lives of others is equivalent to the degree that we have allowed God and others to change us.

These final words are as challenging to me as they may be to you. I decided some time ago never to preach on a subject that hasn't changed my own life first. As God changes me, I can become the means of changing others. Reaching modern and postmodern secular people involves much strategy. But true success is more about who we are in Christ than it is about strategy. Strategy without faith and prayer is empty. On the other hand, if our outreach employs faith and prayer without a coherent strategy, it will often be like a car up on blocks with its wheels spinning aimlessly. The key to touching the heart in a secular, postmodern world is faith and strategy together. Our common sense and our careful planning work hand-in-hand with the power and guidance of the Spirit. One relationship begets another. And by the grace of God, the everlasting gospel will transform an ever-changing world.

# If you appreciated this book, you'll want to read this one also:

**Grounds for Belief**

*Ed Dickerson*

Change is inevitable—except from vending machines.

Times change. Today we live in a decentralized, media-dominated, postmodern world.

The Internet enables the exchange of ideas and information unimagined by previous generations. We're more connected electronically than ever before, but more of us feel isolated and lacking in close friends.

Is there such a thing as truth anymore? Can we tell who's telling the truth?

Ed Dickerson thinks so. He specializes in making Christianity accessible to contemporary audiences. Like the apostle Paul, he'd "rather say five words that everyone can understand and learn from than say ten thousand that sound to others like gibberish" (1 Corinthians 14:19, *The Message*).

Seekers, debaters, the proud, and the humble come to his Grounds for Belief Café.

Come along and eavesdrop on the conversations taking place there. And don't be surprised if they turn philosophical and then spiritual, or if you find grounds for belief that really make sense to you.

Paperback, 145 pages.

ISBN 13: 978-0-8163-2184-1     ISBN 10: 0-8163-2184-1

**Three ways to order:**

1. Local Adventist Book Center®
2. Call 1-800-765-6955
3. Shop AdventistBookCenter.com